TURKEY TODAY
– A European country?

Anthem Press
An imprint of Wimbledon Publishing Company
www.anthempress.com

This edition first published in UK and USA 2004
by ANTHEM PRESS
75–76 Blackfriars Road, London SE1 8HA, UK
or PO Box 9779, London SW19 7ZG, UK
and
244 Madison Ave. #116, New York, NY 10016, USA

Previously published in 2004 in French as *La Turquie Aujord'hui*
© 2004 Encyclopaedia Universalis

Individual chapters © individual contributors 2004

The moral right of the authors has been asserted.

All rights reserved. Without limiting the rights under copyright
reserved above, no part of this publication may be reproduced,
stored or introduced into a retrieval system, or transmitted,
in any form or by any means (electronic, mechanical,
photocopying, recording or otherwise), without
the prior written permission of both the copyright
owner and the above publisher of this book.

British Library Cataloguing in Publication Data
A catalogue record for this book is available from the British
Library.

Library of Congress Cataloging in Publication Data
A catalog record for this book has been requested.

1 3 5 7 9 10 8 6 4 2

ISBN 978 1 84331 172 0 (Hbk)
ISBN 978 1 84331 173 7 (Pbk)

TURKEY TODAY

– A European country?

edited by
Olivier Roy

Anthem Press

List of Contributors	vii
Chronology	ix
Human Rights Conventions ratified by Turkey, Bulgaria and Romania	xiii
INTRODUCTION: TURKEY ON THE ROAD TO EUROPE OLIVIER ROY	1

discussion

TURKEY – A WORLD APART, OR EUROPE'S NEW FRONTIER? OLIVIER ROY	11
TURKEY – A DEMOCRACY UNDER CONTROL? GILLES DORRONSORO	27
THE TURKISH ECONOMY BETWEEN NEO-LIBERALISM AND THE WEIGHT OF STATISM BURCU GÜLTEKIN	39
ISLAM IN TURKEY: A 'SECULAR MUSLIM' STATE ÉLISE MASSICARD	53
TURKEY AND THE EUROPEAN UNION: FROM MIGRATION TO INTEGRATION? VALÉRIE AMIRAUX	67
CAN THE KURDISH QUESTION BE RESOLVED WITHIN EUROPE? HAMIT BOZARSLAN	79

contexts

THE OTTOMAN EMPIRE / ROBERT MANTRAN	**93**
MUSTAFA KEMAL ATATÜRK / ROBERT MANTRAN	**119**
THE GENESIS OF THE IDEA OF EUROPE / JEAN-BAPTISTE DUROSELLE	**131**
THE IDEA OF EUROPE SINCE 1945 / ALFRED GROSSER	**149**
THE ARMENIAN GENOCIDE / CHRISTOPHE CHICLET	**163**
THE CYPRIOT QUESTION / ALI KAZANCIGIL	**173**
MAKARIOS III / EMMANUEL ZAKHOS-PAPAZAKHARIOU	**181**
Bibliography	**185**
Further Internet Resources	**189**
Glossary	**191**
Index	**195**

LIST OF CONTRIBUTORS

Olivier Roy is Director of Research at the Centre National de Recherche Scientifique (CNRS). He recently published *Les illusions du 11 septembre et l'Islam mondialisé*, Seuil, 2002.

Gilles Dorronsoro is Professor of Political Science and Scientific Secretary of the Institut Français d'Études Anatoliennes (IFEA), Istanbul.

Burcu Gültekin was a researcher at the Institut Français d'Études Anatoliennes (IFEA), Istanbul, between 2000 and 2002. She is currently preparing her doctoral thesis in economics at the Institut d'Études Politique (IEP) in Paris.

Élise Massicard is a researcher with the National Centre for Scientific Research (CNRS) in France.

Valérie Amiraux is a researcher at the Centre Universitaire de Recherches Administratives et Politiques de Picardie (CNRS-CURAPP) and currently Marie Curie Fellow at the Robert Schuman Centre for Advanced Studies of the European University Institute in Florence (Italy). She is the author of *Acteurs de l'Islam entre Allemagne et Turquie. Parcours militants et expériences religieuses*, Harmattan, 2001.

Hamit Bozarslan is a lecturer at the École des Hautes Études en Sciences Sociales, Paris.

Robert Mantran (1971–99) was an eminent Historian, specializing in the Ottoman Empire. He also worked with GREPO and as consultant to UNESCO.

Jean-Baptiste Duroselle (1917–94) was Historian, professor in the Sorbonne and the Institute of Political Stuides of Paris.

His publications included *Europe: A History of Its Peoples* (Viking, 1990) and *France and the Nazi Threat: The Collapse of French Diplomacy, 1932–39*, Enigma Books, 2004.

Alfred Grosser eminent journalist and publisher, works with the journal *Science-Po* (Fondation Nationale des Sciences Politiques). His many publications include *Western Alliance: Europe / American Relations*, Alfred A Knopf, 1982 and *L'explication Politiques (Historiques)*, Editions Complexe, 1984. In 1975 he was awarded the peace prize of the German book trade.

Christophe Chiclet is a Historian and journalist, specializing in the Balkans, in particular in Greece and contemporary Macedonia. His publications include *Kosovo: the Trap*, Harmattan, 2000 and *Greek Communists in the War*, Harmattan, 1987.

Ali Kazancigil began his career as a porgramme specialist, editor of *International Social Science,* and then became Director of the Division of Social Science Research and Policy at the Social and Human Sciences Sector (SHS). He had edited many works, including *Comparing Nations: Concepts, Strategies, Substance*, Blackwell, 1994.

Emmanuel Zakhos-Papazakhariou is a respected scholar in the study of Turkey and the Middle East. His publications include Özbayri, K. and Zakhos-Papazakhariou, E, 1976, 'Documents de Tradition Orale desTurcs d'Origine Crétoise', Turcica, VIII (1): 292–346.

CHRONOLOGY

10 August 1920
The Treaty of Sèvres approves the disintegration of the Ottoman Empire and of Turkey.

24 July 1923
The Treaty of Lausanne cancels that of Sèvres and recognises Turkish sovereignty over a territory more or less equivalent to present-day Turkey.

29 October 1923
The foundation of the Turkish Republic, of which Mustafa Kemal is immediately elected president.

3 March 1924
Abolition of the caliphate.

30 April 1924
Adoption of the Constitution, which institutes a parliamentary system of government with a single chamber, elected by direct vote for a term of four years.

1934
Women obtain the right to vote.

10 November 1938
Death of Mustafa Kemal.

1945
Neutral at the beginning of the war, Turkey symbolically enters alongside the Allies.

1946–1950
Institution of the multiparty system.

18 February 1952
Turkey joins NATO.

18 May 1954
Turkey ratifies the European Convention on Human Rights and Fundamental Freedoms.

25 March 1957
The Treaty of Rome establishes the European Common Market.

27 May 1960
Military coup d'état against the civilian government, accused of betraying Kemalism and seeking to diminish the central role of the army.

12 September 1963
First Association Agreement between the European Economic Community and Turkey (known as the Ankara Agreement), laying down the fundamental objectives of the association such as ongoing and balanced reinforcement of trade and economic relations, and the establishment of a customs union.

12 March 1971
Military *pronunciamiento* establishing a strong government.

July–August 1974
Turkey occupies the northern half of Cyprus.

12 September 1980
Military coup d'état.

1983
Electoral victory of the Motherland Party (ANAP) lead by Turgut Özal brings about the re-democratisation of the regime.

14 April 1987
Turkey officially becomes a candidate for European Community membership.

18 December 1989 and 5 February 1990
The European Commission, followed by the Council, declare that Turkey is eligible to apply for membership – but refuse its admission.

June 1993
The European Council held in Copenhagen defines the criteria for admission to the European Union.

15 December 1995
The European Parliament ratifies the customs union treaty signed in March by the 15 member states and Turkey, due to come into force following the adoption of democratic reforms by the Turkish Parliament.

24 December 1995
Victory of the Islamist Refah Party (RP) at the parliamentary elections.

12/13 December 1997
At the Luxembourg summit, negotiations concerning accession are begun with all the countries requesting membership except Turkey, which perceives this as a national humiliation.

16 January 1998
The Constitutional Court dissolves the RP for violating the principle of secularity.

4 March 1998
The Commission adopts a *Communication* on 'European Strategy for Turkey'. Harmonisation of legislation and the adoption of the Community *acquis* (common terms and conditions) are among the principal elements of the pre-accession strategy for Turkey.

June 1998
In Cardiff, Turkey is not admitted for accession at the same time as the countries of the former Eastern Europe, but the Commission proposes to help the country prepare its candidacy.

13 December 1999
The European Council held in Helsinki marks the definitive acceptance of Turkey among the candidate countries.

9 February 2000
The PKK officially announces – as requested by its leader Abdullah Öcalan – that it repudiates armed struggle. A dialogue is begun in order to find a 'peaceful solution' to the Kurdish problem.

November 2000
Turkey is hit by a serious economic crisis.

3 November 2002
The AKP, successor of the RP party, led by Recep Tayyip Erdogan, wins the parliamentary elections.

12 December 2002
At the European Council held in Copenhagen, the EU member states ratify the enlargement of the Union to 25 members. However, the EU postpones its decision on opening negotiations regarding Turkey's accession to December 2004, insisting that Turkey respect the three Copenhagen criteria.

11 March 2003
Recep Tayyip Erdogan is given a mandate to form the government.

15/20 November 2003
Violent attacks hit the Jewish community and British interests in Turkey.

December 2004
The EU announces its decision to open negotiations with Turkey regarding its accession.

HUMAN RIGHTS CONVENTIONS

Conventions ratified by the candidate countries in the domain of human rights:

Conventions and Protocols	Bulgaria	Romania	Turkey
European Convention on Human Rights	●	●	●
Protocol No. 1 (property rights)	●	●	●
Protocol No. 4 (freedom of circulation, etc.)	●	●	●
Protocol No. 6 (death penalty)	●	●	● Not yet notified to the Council of Europe
Protocol No. 7 (double jeopardy: a person cannot be charged twice for the same offence)	●	●	●
European Convention on the Prevention of Torture	●	●	●
European Social Charter (revised)	●	●	●
Framework Convention for the Protection of National Minorities	●	●	●
International Covenant on Civil and Political Rights	●	●	●
Optional Protocol to the International Covenant on Civil and Political Rights (individuals' communication rights)	●	●	●
Second Optional Protocol to the International Covenant on Civil and Political Rights (death penalty)	●	●	●
International Covenant on Economic, Social and Cultural Rights	●	●	●
Convention Against Torture	●	●	●
International Convention on the Elimination of all Forms of Racial Discrimination	●	●	●
Convention on the Elimination of all Forms of Discrimination Against Women	●	●	●
Optional Protocol to the Convention on the Elimination of all Forms of Discrimination Against Women	●	●	●
Convention on the Rights of the Child	●	●	●

Source: European Commission, *2003 Regular Report on the Progress of Turkey towards Accession* (December 2003).

xiv

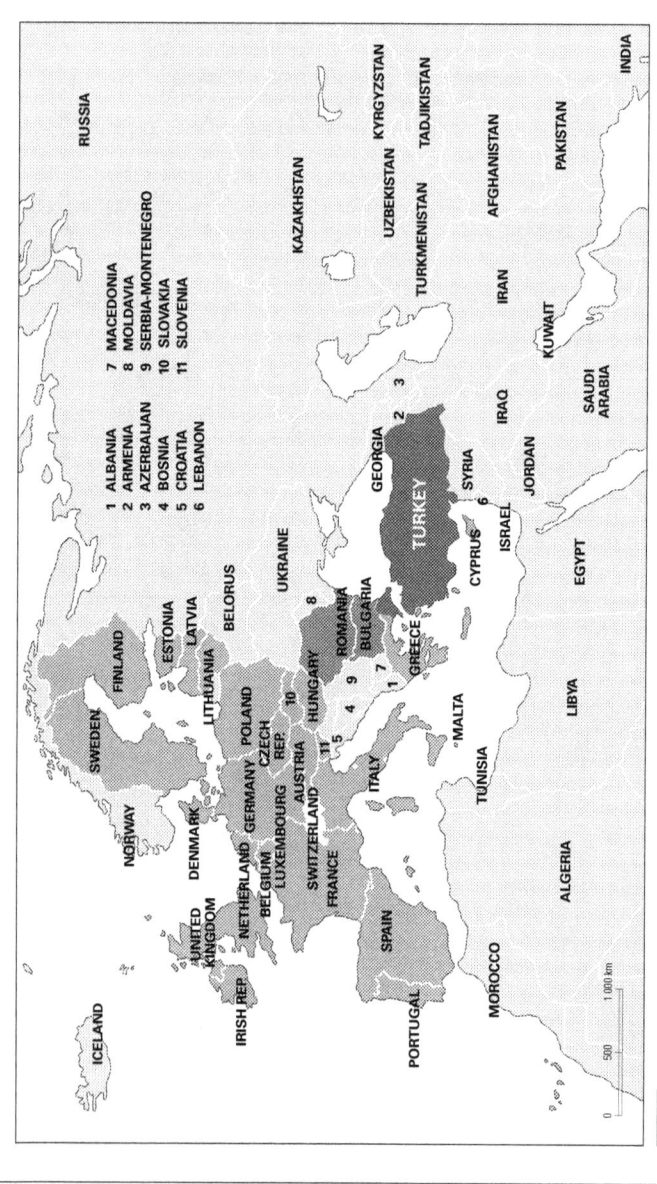

Turkey: between East and West

INTRODUCTION:
TURKEY ON THE ROAD TO EUROPE

Where, we might ask, is Turkey – in Asia or in Europe? The answer is, of course: between the two. Yet a decision has to be made, for in the European Union one cannot remain on the confines, in some sort of buffer or in-between status. You are either in or you are out. Turkey's application in 1987 to join the European Union means that one decision has already been taken – Turkey considers itself European.

This position follows perfectly logically from the genuine revolution brought about by Mustafa Kemal Atatürk, who in the 1920s deliberately chose to wrest Turkey from its Muslim past. The importance of Atatürk's cultural sea-change cannot be stressed enough, from the spectacular change in alphabet, adopting the use of Roman characters, to the ukases imposing Western-style dress – not to mention less well-known measures such as requiring civil servants to attend Saturday evening balls with their wives dressed in sleeveless gowns, something that in the far-flung provinces of Anatolia must have seemed like a form of nudity. Until the 1980s, Turkish radio broadcast nothing but European classical music, without giving any airtime to the oriental music that was so popular in Paris, well beyond the predominantly Muslim neighbourhood of Barbès. The reforms went through, and not only thanks to the bayonets of the federal police – although naturally these also played a role – but because for the majority of the population there was no real alternative to this concept of modernity. Any resistance seemed merely to hark back to the past.

On today's political spectrum only the extreme right-wing Turkish nationalists openly oppose the option to join Europe, and they do so not out of nostalgia for the Ottoman Empire or the Muslim Caliphate, but because they have all too readily made their own the chauvinistic nationalism that is a legacy of westernization. Yet this nationalism is shared by the army as well as by the nationalist left (of former Prime Minister Bülent Ecevit), who have never explained how one can reconcile such a punctilious nationalism with the surrender of sovereignty implied by accession to Europe. The Islamists, for their part, have not only renounced their traditional opposition to Europe, but have even discovered that there are advantages to be gained from a Europe that allows them to escape from the oppressive dominance of the army over the political system.

Of course there are all sorts of motives behind this interest in Europe. The social elites feel that culturally they are European. The great Turkish universities are of very high calibre, and some of them, like Bilkent – Ankara's leading university – explicitly follow the model of American universities. The managerial class, dynamic and independent of the political sphere, is turned resolutely toward the West. Moreover, the Turkish diplomatic corps (one of the last outposts in which French is still the preferred language of diplomacy) seems to consider its sole vocation is to secure the country's entry into Europe. The army, a pillar of NATO, sees the Middle East only as a source of trouble and not as a zone of influence or of future prospects: it wants to turn its back on the region and hitch its fate to Europe, all the while brandishing the national flag. This simply stirs up the debate over a Europe of the nations versus a federal Europe. The lower classes are somewhat more ambiguous in their attitude toward Europe, for they are less fascinated by the cultural model than by access to its labour market – an attitude that is not without its problems.

If by making its application in 1987 Turkey has officially decided in favour of Europe, Europe has been less keen to return the favour. The European Union, through its

Commission, accepted the principle of Turkey's candidacy in 1989, and the Council followed suit in 1990. Since then, however, the EU has interminably blown hot and cold, delaying and confirming the candidacy over the course of various European summits without ever setting a precise date. In this way Europe is continually reopening a question that the Turks consider well and truly resolved – is Turkey really European?

Of course Europe has defined very precise criteria for accession, which apply to Turkey just as they do to other candidates. They are concerned essentially with the reforms necessary for the institutional workings of a democratic state under the rule of law, and with respect for human rights. Running parallel to these is the need to resolve the remaining dispute with Greece, from the Aegean Sea to Cyprus.

Underlying the modernisation of institutions, there is also the problem of the economic development of Turkey: How can a country which in terms of population ranks between Germany and France, with a working class whose importance is unparallelled elsewhere in Europe, and which has already been the source of significant labour migration, enter the Union without releasing an enormous stream of migrants? The latter would be ill-received by European popular opinion, already sceptical of the prospects for integrating those Turks currently living in Europe. The size of Turkey makes it impossible to envisage the sort of massive financial aid that allowed little Portugal within a few years to reach the economic level of the rest of Europe.

And finally, and perhaps most importantly, European public opinion as well as politicians are troubled by other questions that are never addressed directly with the Turkish negotiators: can a European country, a member state of the Union, be Muslim?

It is these questions that we address in this book, approaching each of the major themes in Turkey's domestic politics today from the perspective of membership in the European Union.

The first task is to examine the place of Turkey in history and geography. How does its position between Europe and Asia make the country into a bridge, or a bridgehead, from Asia to Europe or from Europe to Asia? Did the reforms of Atatürk succeed in lifting the weight of the Ottoman Empire? In fact, as the Iraqi War demonstrated in 2003, Turkey does not look to the East except to shut itself off from the conflicts that trouble that region. It does not take part in the Israeli-Palestinian conflict, and allies itself with Israel while simply ignoring the Palestinians, who enjoy – in Turkey as in Europe – a great deal of sympathy in public opinion but without any specific political commitment.

If Turkey patrols its eastern borders, it is primarily because of the Kurdish question – and in this regard it is fully in harmony with a deep-rooted European idea: from the East there can come nothing but trouble. The question, of course, is: where does the East begin – within Turkey itself, or at the borders of Iraq and Iran? It is interesting to note that the terrorist attacks that hit Istanbul in November 2003 were committed in the name of al-Qaeda by Turkish nationals who were predominantly Kurds. Turkey's entire strategy today is directed, in effect, at a convergence with Europe, with the exception of the handling of the Kurdish question.

But what about internal factors?

Turkish institutions are quite unique, as Gilles Dorronsoro demonstrates. Certainly it is a democracy, but an authoritarian democracy, in which the 'underlying State' – that is, the army and the inner core of the government – defines the limits beyond which one cannot go, oversees the elected governments, and can ban parties in the name of the secular principle or of national unity.

It is true that it is not so long ago (in the 1970s) that the army withdrew from the political scene in Greece, Spain or Portugal. But in Turkey, the weight of the army is felt not only in times of *putsch*, as in 1981. It is deeply inscribed in the institutions and in hearts and minds, for it is tied to nationalism and perhaps also, among many secular Turkish intellectuals, to the idea that democracy and secularity are still fragile in a regional context that is at the very least still in agitation.

At the same time, it is this 'underlying State' that also seeks to join Europe and is ultimately transformed by its desire for European membership. Accession to the European Union may contribute to the perpetuation of a Kemalism that still seems to many to be a historical stroke of luck, while at the same time stripping it of the ideological and institutional straightjacket that renders it incapable of adapting to a changing world. The reforms are being carried out – although from time to time there are a few spectacular steps backward, as is evident from the arrest of certain journalists or deputies. But they *are* being carried out.

Moreover, the Turkish economy – as Burcu Gültekin's analysis shows – is not the economy of a Third World country. Built up thanks to protectionist barriers, a class of entrepreneurial leaders has emerged today that is sufficiently solid to demand the end of that same protectionism, gradually abolished since Turgut Özal become Prime Minster in 1983. They want less government and more market and openness. But the social disparities, inflation, the weight of the working class, and an endemic corruption suggest instead that Turkey is functioning at two speeds: the upper level has become Europeanised, while the rest are struggling to survive.

On the other hand, the Kurdish question remains the most sensitive topic and undoubtedly, together with that of Cyprus, constitutes the real obstacle to Turkey's integration into Europe. Yet, as Hamit Bozarslan shows, the 'underlying State' cannot but acknowledge the Kurdish fact (and especially their language). However, the mad adventure of the PKK (the Kurdistan Workers' Party) has given rise to disillusionment and bitterness among a population tired of civil war, frustrated by the chauvinistic authoritarianism of the state, and dreaming of models other than that of a centralising, intolerant Jacobin state or that of an independence promoted by militants for whom, by all accounts, democracy is not the first concern.

Between the Marxist nationalism of the PKK and the authoritarian state, Europe offers a range of models, from Catalonia to Scotland, which could help to reconcile Kurdish identity and the Turkish republic. In fact, the evolution of the Kemalist model and the decline of ultra-nationalism have created the conditions for a means of coexistence to emerge between the Turkish state and the Kurds. But as long as the Kurdish question continues to be criminalised, nothing will happen. Yet the development of a Kurdish entity in the northern part of Iraq, thanks to US military occupation, brings the risk of increased tensions between the Turkish army and all Westerners, both Europeans and Americans.

Immigration likewise remains a sensitive subject, although more so in Europe than in Turkey. The Turkish elites who knock at the gates of Europe are oblivious to their emigrant compatriots, for they feel remote from them both culturally and socially. The state certainly does its job: it sends and finances teachers (but also mullahs) to keep Turks living in Europe within the bosom of their homeland. But the elite does not feel any kinship with the emigrant working class, which is far more traditionalist than the residents of Istanbul and Ankara, practises a strong endogamy, and professes an Islam that strikes many Europeans as a bad omen for the integration of Turkey into Europe. Yet this emigration – as Valérie Amiraux demonstrates – is not a true reflection of Turkey but has its own internal logic, and its traditionalism is less a sign of the importation of Anatolian values than a form of reactive adaptation to a westernisation that has already made an impact.

There remains the question of Islam. Although a secular republic, Turkey is a profoundly Muslim country in which Sunni Islam is actually the state religion by default, because it is the only religion taken into account, and often even controlled, by the political powers. The Turkish form of secularity must in any case be placed in perspective, as Élise Massicard proposes. But this is also true of Sweden or Denmark, or even Great Britain, where the Queen is the head of the Church. The real question, then, is less about institutional secularity than about the role that Islam plays in Turkish society.

No matter which way we look at it, we always come back to the identity and complexity of a society. One can easily reform institutions, but what about a society? Certainly Atatürk did it, but does the return of the religious factor not indicate precisely the limits of social engineering when it comes to transforming a people? Élise Massicard shows that far from being the expression of a tradition and a rejection of modernity, Islam in Turkey – complex and diversified as it is – has on the contrary adapted itself to this modernisation. The evolution of Turkish Islam today depends not on the edicts of the state or on the *fatwas* of the *ulema*, but rather on the daily life and religious practice of each and every person. In short, what is needed for Turkey to become fully European is perhaps just a little more time. But time can also fan the flames of frustration, and gives everyone a pretext not to tackle the fundamental questions – the very ones that we wish to address in this book.

discussion

TURKEY – A WORLD APART,
OR EUROPE'S NEW FRONTIER? **11**
OLIVIER ROY

TURKEY – A DEMOCRACY UNDER CONTROL? **27**
GILLES DORRONSORO

THE TURKISH ECONOMY BETWEEN NEO-LIBERALISM
AND THE WEIGHT OF STATISM **39**
BURCU GÜLTEKIN

ISLAM IN TURKEY: A 'SECULAR MUSLIM' STATE **53**
ÉLISE MASSICARD

TURKEY AND THE EUROPEAN UNION:
FROM MIGRATION TO INTEGRATION? **67**
VALÉRIE AMIRAUX

CAN THE KURDISH
QUESTION BE RESOLVED WITHIN EUROPE? **79**
HAMIT BOZARSLAN

TURKEY – A WORLD APART, OR EUROPE'S NEW FRONTIER?

THE PHANTOM OF THE EMPIRE

Turkey is located at the geographical crossroads between Europe and Asia, but it is also a crossroads between extremely diverse, and sometimes contradictory, cultural and political models. Along with its true capital (Byzantium/Constantinople/Istanbul), Turkey was for fifteen centuries the centre of empires (Byzantine and then Ottoman) that were by definition multi-ethnic and subject to variable borders depending on conquests and rebellions. These empires certainly had religious legitimacy, essential for reigning over such diverse populations, but they also knew how to manage their external alliances with a conservative pragmatism that eventually became ossified.

Modern Turkey, which is less than a century old, has deliberately broken with this heritage. Even if the Ottomans were the first to launch a process of westernization, with the *Tanzimat*, a period of reform inaugurated in 1839, it is impossible to overstate the importance of Atatürk, who brutally rejected the imperial model in favour of the nation-state, demanding above all homogeneity in terms of population, territory, history and language, barricaded behind near-sacred frontiers and defending national interests defined primarily in military terms. In a sense, this is the paradox of Turkey: westernization, at once coerced and successful, led the country to close in on itself and turn away to a certain extent from its neighbours in the region, from the Balkans to the Middle East and the Caucasus. Moreover, if NATO warmly welcomed Turkey among its ranks in 1952, it is because the West saw it as a rampart (or a buffer, if you prefer) against the Soviet enemy, but also against a Middle East that the West wished to keep as far away as possible. Once the centre of the Middle East, Turkey now became the edge of Europe.

But today, the pinnacle of this westernization, admission to the European Union, presupposes the abandonment of the very model that had made it possible – the Kemalist nation-state, one that is Jacobin and lay, authoritarian and fiercely nationalist – in favour of a Europe that looks more and more like a vague federal empire, with its fluid identity (whence its capacity to admit new members), fluctuating borders, and a foreign policy limited to what each member is willing to contribute to the common pot. Since 1987 Turkey has been knocking insistently at the door that Europe occasionally opens slightly and then closes again.

In the end, though, does Turkey need Europe?

Turkish foreign policy is certainly determined by geostrategic constraints (the Straits, for example), but it depends even more upon the paradigms that help define Turkey itself. If we take the Ottoman model as the reference point, then Turkey has a Balkan, Caucasian, and Middle Eastern identity, but can accommodate minorities (the Kurds) on its own territory. If, on the other hand, we take the strictly Kemalist model, then Turkey should not concern itself with anything beyond its own borders, but should reject everything that threatens its national unity (the Kurdish conflict is a perverse effect of this Kemalist rigidity). If we adopt the pan-Turkist position, then the new areas of Central Asia (where no Ottoman ever governed) form the horizon for a Turkey that no longer has any need for Europe. From the perspective of the Islamists, Turkey ought to mobilise the religious legitimacy conferred by the Caliphate and take back the leadership of the *umma*, or Muslim community. In reality, it is the subjective ideological vision of the country that defines its geostrategy, and not the other way around. Geostrategy, in Turkey as elsewhere, is none other than the constraint or the mission that the country wishes to assume.

The Solitary Birth of Modern Turkey (1922-1945)

The Kemalist revolution invented modern Turkey by an explicit break with the Ottoman Empire – ethnic homogeneity versus multi-ethnicity: a strong, centralised state in opposition to the power of notables and local authorities, a purely national legitimacy instead of the Islamic Caliphate, the refusal to consider itself a great power in order to focus on defending a territory that although reduced in size was to be inviolable. In essence, it was a question of transforming a defeat into a renaissance. The dismemberment of the Ottoman Empire that had begun in the eighteenth century was finished off brutally by the victory of the Allies in 1918. The Treaty of Sèvres (1920) made Turkey into a sort of equivalent of Austria – a rump state without much of an identity.

The war waged by Atatürk to have the Treaty of Sèvres annulled was not at all based on a nostalgia for the Ottoman era but, on the contrary, on the desire to break with all references to the past by playing fully the card of the modern nation-state: one people, incarnate in one language, one territory, one state, one national army. This quest for homogeneity led Atatürk without regret to let go of the territories populated by Arabs. But he also renounced explicitly all pan-Turkism, which had been the driving force behind some of his colleagues in the Young Turks movement. The nationalism of Atatürk was linguistic, not racial: a Turkish-speaking Kurd experienced no discrimination in his political career. This primacy of the political bond came up against the concept of religious minorities, especially those protected by the Treaty of Lausanne of 1923, which put an end to the conflict with Greece. If the Jews, for their part, were perfectly integrated – no doubt because they in no way represented a potential bridgehead for another state – the Greek and Armenian Christians who became Turkish citizens were *de facto* excluded from the upper ranks of the army and the political establishment.

Atatürk's foreign policy was highly isolationist, but also non-conflictual, even if tensions with Greece remained strong. Turkey never challenged the borders with Greece that had been imposed by the Treaty of Lausanne, even if it systematically pleaded (and continues to do so) that the Aegean Sea not become a 'Greek lake'. The only territorial demands made by Turkey concerned the Sanjak of Alexandretta, an administrative district annexed to Syria under the French mandate. On this matter, however, Turkey received satisfaction in 1939. The question of Cyprus (then under British administration) had not yet arisen. Turkey scrupulously respected the letter, if not the spirit, of the Treaty of Lausanne and accepted, by the Montreux Convention (1936), the free passage of foreign ships through the Straits (Bosporus and the Dardanelles). Turkey voluntarily excluded itself from the system of axes and alliances formed between the two world wars, maintaining a chilly coexistence with the USSR and Greece, good relations with Iran and the Western powers (French and British) controlling its borders with the Arab world, while breaking off its privileged relations with Germany and affirming its neutrality during World War II.

TURKEY, PILLAR OF NATO

This autarchy disappeared after World War II. In February 1945 Turkey declared war, as a pure formality, against Nazi Germany, in order to participate in the Potsdam Conference and in the founding of the UN. The USSR undertook at the same moment to exert pressure on Ankara to modify the statute concerning the Straits and the delineation of their common border. Turkey thereupon requested the support of the United States, which in 1947 inaugurated the tradition of direct financial and military support that endures to this day. Turkey, by sending troops to Korea to fight alongside the Americans under the UN flag (1950) and then by joining NATO (1952) clearly chose sides – in favour of the West, in opposition to the USSR.

Paradoxically, this choice did not make it into a regional power. Turkey instead kept a very low profile in the region, all the more so because it recognised the state of Israel right from the start (1948) and thus broke ranks with the Arab countries. The tensions with Greece were neutralized, although they did not disappear, by virtue of the two countries' membership of NATO. Furthermore, the crisis of 1955 led to a final exchange of populations between Greece and Turkey. The border with the USSR was transformed into an impenetrable barrier. Finally, Turkey's relations with an independent Syria turned sour, for Damascus never recognized the surrender of the Alexandretta Sandjak. Turkey thus became a faithful ally of the United States – the Turkish contingent in the Korean War suffered the greatest losses after those of the US and British troops.

GREECE, THE BELOVED ENEMY

If tensions with Greece were easily contained within the framework of NATO, under American influence they complicated relations between Turkey and Europe. Some say, after all, that if Giscard d'Estaing supported Greece's candidacy in 1974, it was above all in order to block that of Turkey. The Greco-Turkish tension is often presented as a thousand-year-old conflict. But beyond the symbolic value of history (Constantinople against the Ottomans, the Cross against the Crescent), the real opposition only began in 1920 as the confrontation between two nation-states over the control of a territory and of a sea.

Previously, Greece had been but one nation among many trying to shake off the Ottoman yoke (in 1914, Greece nearly joined the German camp and thus that of Ottoman Turkey). But the violence of the war of 1920-21, the massacres and the displacement of peoples left a lasting mark, for this could truly be said to have been a vital combat for both countries. The Treaty of Sèvres had made Greece into an Anatolian power by giving it the Aegean coast along with Izmir. For the Greeks, to lose the war meant to be forced definitively out of an East in which classical Greek and then Byzantine culture had once flourished. Not to have control over its own coastline signified for Turkey that it was from now on just a rump state thrust back upon an Orient from which its new elites wished to escape.

Theoretically, the areas in dispute after the 1923 Treaty of Lausanne were limited to a few rocky islands. It was the series of decisions taken by the Greeks to remilitarize the islands off the coast of Turkey, to extend their territorial waters and their airspace, thereby transforming the Aegean Sea into a 'Greek lake', that reignited tensions with Turkey (even if Greece did not apply the restrictions on movement that it believed it had the right to impose). Then in 1974 the Greco-Turkish conflict was played out in miniature on the island of Cyprus. An Ottoman possession yielded to the British in 1876, with one-third of its population Turkish and two-thirds Greek, the island gained its independence in 1959 following a guerrilla movement led by Greeks who wanted *enosis* – that is, union with Greece – but it was never able to achieve political stability.

In 1974, an extreme rightist Greek movement, supported by the military dictatorship then in power in Athens, overthrew the regime of President Makarios, proclaimed reunion with Greece, and attacked the island's Turkish population. Turkey reacted by invading the island. Partition followed. One third of the island was transferred to Turkish hands, who established the Turkish Republic of Northern Cyprus, which was not recognized by the international community, while the Greek population fled to the south, which maintained the fiction of the continuity of the Cypriot state since it had achieved independence.

Like so many virtual conflicts, the one between Greece and Turkey never led to an outright war, but each acted as if such a possibility should never be excluded. The leaders knew that actual conflict was impossible: the peoples did not wish it, and although the actual dispute has today been reduced and is negotiable, there remains a posture of hostility and of immanent danger on both sides Recently, the Turkish army evinced its opposition to the overtures concerning Cyprus made by Turkish Prime Minister Recep Tayyip Erdogan. In November 2003 the Greek army was reorganized, and on the one hand considerably reduced its forces (a sign of the absence of any real threat), while on the other hand it redeployed its troops under the evident impression that the only perceived threat was from Turkey. Here the weight of history, state nationalism and religious identities reinforce each other: in Greece as in Turkey, religion still figures on the national identity card.

THE KURDS, THORNS IN THE SIDE

On an international level, the Kurdish question would appear on the radar only if the Kurds, who live in four different countries (Turkey, Iraq, Iran, Syria), were able to set up a coordinated movement to create a larger independent Kurdistan. That is far from likely. But it cannot be said to be a purely internal affair either, for the Kurdish question determines Turkey's entire regional policy. In effect, the neighbouring countries (Iran, Iraq and Syria) have a lever they can use with Turkey, for they can either give asylum to the PKK (the Kurdistan Workers' Party, which is the chief weapon of the armed struggle in Turkey) or they can expel them. This in turn obliges Ankara to pay close attention to the internal affairs of neighbouring countries, and even to intervene directly (as with military operations in Iraqi Kurdistan in the 1990s, and pressure on Syria to expel Abdullah Öcalan, leader of the PKK, in 1999).

The Europeans, at times sympathetic to the Kurds, at other times afraid of the regional implications of a potential escalation of the conflict, demand that the question be settled, noting the security threat and the violations of human rights that result from their repression. The PKK very astutely made the city of Brussels the focal point of their demonstrations.

THE CRISIS OF THE KEMALIST PARADIGM AND THE FALL OF THE USSR

The military coup d'état in 1983, aimed both at the Islamists and at the extreme left, revealed the extreme polarisation of the system and the demise of the Kemalist model. The prime minister, and later president (1983-93), Turgut Özal – a former Islamist with Kurdish roots who was supported by the military – oversaw the transition. He understood that the Kemalist model would inevitably be called into question, but that the internal and external political dimensions were closely linked and depended on the invention of new paradigms. For instance, he broke the taboo against the word 'Kurd' (he spoke openly of the Kurds and of the Kurdish language), and launched a programme of development in the southeast in the wake of military operations. He openly declared himself to be a practising Muslim. He privatised the economy as well, breaking with another fundamental principle of Kemalism. But above all, Özal profited from a spectacular event – the fall of the USSR in 1991, which opened up a new strategic space for Turkey.

To have held on to Kemalism would have meant paralysis. But if there was to be movement, what new strategic vision could be formulated? In fact, the crisis of the Kemalist movement and the fall of the USSR reactivated other paradigms for the nature of Turkey. If these did not necessarily provide a real alternative, they did allow the system to evolve. One's view of the national interests of Turkey depends, in effect, on one's definition of Turkish identity. Turkey is not faced with a permanent or structural threat (as India or Pakistan, the relations between which are tense). If Greece is often perceived as the principal enemy, it may be a nuisance but is not a serious threat. Nor is Turkey's stubbornness in the matter of the Armenian question tied to a concrete danger, but to a question of identity. Finally, the only true threat to the territorial integrity of Turkey – namely the challenge from the Kurds – is not linked to any action by a neighbouring country (none of them genuinely wants to see the secession of the Kurds from Turkey).

The Turkish political actors repositioned themselves in around 1990 in terms of their conception of the Turkish nation and of the new international environment. The army and the large centrist parties are at the same time nationalist – in the Kemalist sense – pro-European, and Atlanticist. The right-wing nationalists (MHP) are strongly anticommunist, pan-Turkist, and wary of binding alliances (such as NATO and Europe). The Kemalist left is also very nationalistic, but is also violently anti-Islamist and intractable on the Kurdish question – a position that aligns it with the army. The members of the Refah (Welfare) Party, an extreme Islamist party dissolved in 1998, sought to promote an Ottoman model wherein Turkey would concentrate on its regional surroundings, beginning with the Middle East, and thus would privilege relations with the Muslim world in general and Arab nations in particular.

Islamists of Refah and pan-Turkists can thus make common cause on a certain number of themes: support for Muslims in the former Soviet republics, and Euroscepticism, for instance. But the Islamists are more open on the Kurdish question, and paradoxically also on Cyprus and Armenia, for on these subjects the army is closer to the extreme right and to the Republican People's Party (CHP, the centre-left party of Ecevit), which remains strongly nationalist. The 1990s also brought about an important change in the Islamists: the Justice and Development Party (AK), which won the elections of November 2002, no longer has the same vision as Refah: it has become much more pro-European, in favour of a withdrawal from the Middle East and of an agreement on Cyprus. But business circles (represented by the powerful TÜSIAD) have their own vision of foreign policy – pragmatic in nature, it tends to insist on the European nature of Turkey.

THE FAILURE OF THE NEW '-ISMS'

The new '-isms' developed in university and journalistic milieux as well as within the ideological parties, such as the extreme right or Refah. Although they have had considerable impact on the public, they simply helped politicians make speeches adapted to their audiences rather than changing the foreign policy of Turkey, especially since the 'underlying State' (the army and certain authorities such as the ministry of justice) never accepted these new models.

The Brief Illusions of Pan-Turkism

Developed at the beginning of the twentieth century as an alternative to Ottomanism, pan-Turkism posits that there is an ethnic unity in the Turkic world that must become a political reality. The pan-Turkists do not hesitate to 'Turkify' other peoples (Chechens and Japanese are regularly told that they are related). A creation of Kemal Atatürk, pan-Turkism has always been influential in university circles. Moreover, Istanbul has always attracted liberation movements in exile, such as the East Turkestan movement (that is, of the Uighurs of China's Xinjiang region).

The fall of the USSR gave a new dynamism to pan-Turkism. The members of the university of Marmara elaborated a common Latin alphabet for the Turkic languages of the former Soviet Union. The Gülen movement set up a network of Turkish schools wherever it could. But the movement slowly petered out. It met with no interest among those who might have been concerned, for Central Asia is dominated by nationalism, not by pan-Turkism. The Turkish government did develop a cooperation programme with the countries of Central Asia, but has not picked up on this theme, and in any case does not have the resources necessary for such an ambitious policy.

The Quiet Return of Ottomanism

Özal pushed Turkey to get involved in regional crises, appealing to the country's Ottoman heritage. The Islamists did likewise, in the hope of finding a synthesis between Islam and Turkish identity. But few of the neighbouring countries were ready to accept such a 'return of Ottomanism'. It is therefore as part of the international community that Turkey played an effective, but discreet, role in the Balkans. On the other hand, this return of Ottomanism made an impression on Turkish public opinion, which rediscovered its own diversity that had been obscured by Kemalism. Everyone suddenly recalled a Caucasian grandmother or a Bosnian great-uncle.

In the Shadow of the Caliph: Pan-Islamism

When Necmettin Erbakan became Prime Minister in 1996, he tried to pursue a policy of rapprochement with the Arab world, but failed for two reasons: the Turkish army was opposed to any change in the alliance with Israel, and the Arab countries were wary of Turkey, as was evident from the humiliating failure of Erbakan's visit to Libya. This Muslim alternative was in any case an illusion, as became clear from the effort to create a sort of Muslim common market. The AK, which took the place of Erbakan's Refah party, in any case rejected any Islamic option in foreign policy and turned its focus once again towards Europe.

Curiously, the prudence of the Islamist parties had not opened the path to the development of radical autonomous Islamic currents. There were certainly some Turkish networks prepared to join the jihad in the Caucasus, but if we look at their numbers in relation to the overall population of Turkey, the Turkish contribution to 'international terrorism' is extremely small. A few volunteers served in Chechnya and in Bosnia, but no Turk was ever officially found among the ranks of al-Qaeda, even if the attacks in Istanbul in November 2003 reveal that some ties exist.

TURKEY AS A REGIONAL ACTOR

The fall of the USSR did little to benefit Turkey in terms of its own power game, except in Transcaucasia (in relation to Georgia, Armenia and Azerbaijan). The Turks faithfully supported Azerbaijan's ultranationalist regime led by Abulfaz Elchibey (1991–93), but the experience was disastrous (defeat by the Armenians, a climate of civil war, tensions with Moscow). The rise to power of Heydar Aliev in 1993 was wrongly perceived as the return of a pro-Russian regime in Baku, and certain Turkish services found themselves implicated in the attempts, always unsuccessful, to destabilize the regime. It would be years before minimal confidence would be restored, largely because Azerbaijan threw itself into the arms of the Americans. It was the United States that gave the real impetus.

In Georgia, likewise with US blessing, the Turks launched a programme of military cooperation.

Relations with Armenia obviously remain very cold as a result of the taboos and silences about the past, but Ankara would prefer to improve relations – something that Azerbaijan for its part refuses. The Armenian campaign to get western parliaments to acknowledge the genocide of 1915 exasperates the Turks, who nevertheless can see the votes lining up (the European Parliament, the US Congress and the French Parliament). However, Turkey took an important step (again as a result of American action) when the decision was made to construct the Baku-Ceyhan oil pipeline, which directly connects the Caspian Sea with the Mediterranean, bypassing Russia.

If, on balance, Turkey has considerably extended its sphere of diplomatic action after the dissolution of the USSR, however, it has never – with the exception of the Caucasus (that is, of Azerbaijan) – acted on its own in this new regional environment, but always in the context of international missions (UN, OSCE, NATO, ISAF in Afghanistan) or of regional organisations (Black Sea Treaty, Economic Cooperation Organisation). It also refused, after much hesitation, to act solely on grounds of its strategic alliance with the United States during the campaign against Iraq in 2003. Turkey's politics have become diversified and have grown more complex, but they have not fundamentally changed.

THE ANKARA–WASHINGTON–TEL AVIV AXIS

Conceived initially within the terms of NATO, the alliance between Ankara and Washington increasingly became more of a bilateral and privileged one, especially in the military domain (Turkey receives one billion dollars from Washington per year).

In relation to Israel, Turkey has always refused not only to identify with the Arab rejection but even to associate itself with individual condemnations of Israel. Significantly, there was no massive exodus of Jews from Turkey to Israel. This benevolent attitude was transformed at the end of the 1980s into a true strategic alliance, founded upon military agreements that, for example, allow the Israeli air force to train in Turkey. There was talk then of an alliance against Iran and Arab nationalism.

Yet even if Turkey never hesitated to distance itself, it has always maintained proper relations with the Islamic republic of Iran. Discussions on Iran's supplying Turkey with gas and petrol were thus never disrupted. Alongside Iran and Pakistan, Turkey in 1985 became a founding member of the Economic Cooperation Organisation, the seat of which is in Tehran, and which was intended to serve as a link between Europe and Asia. Similarly, Turkey refused to allow its territory to be used by the US Army for the invasion of Iraq, giving rise to a serious rift with Washington. In truth, Turkey has never appeared an unfailing ally of the United States except within a multilateral context (UN, NATO, OSCE, ISAF). It is clear, therefore, that if the Kemalist model has weakened, no truly alternative foreign policy has emerged in Turkey, only an adaptation to a new environment.

TURKEY AND THE EUROPEAN UNION: TIME TO CHOOSE?

The first agreement of association between Turkey and Europe dates back to 1963, but it was in 1987 that Turkey submitted a formal request for accession to the European Community, thereby starting what would prove to be a recurring cycle. Europeans – while congratulating Turkey on its progress and encouraging it further – regularly set aside the request without rejecting it outright, but always adding new conditions.

After a rebuff at the European summit in Luxembourg in 1997, the Helsinki summit in 1999 accepted Turkey's candidacy in principle. The criteria were refined at the Copenhagen summit in 2002. The conditions have to do with reinforcing human rights and democracy (abolition of the death penalty, reduction of the political role of the army) as well as with the resolution of the Kurdish question and of the tensions over Cyprus and the Aegean Sea. The Turks have regularly taken steps forward (on the death penalty, the use of the Kurdish language), with occasional standstills (over Cyprus), all the while expecting Brussels to reciprocate.

But the root of the problem is that the real reasons for Europe's reticence are never stated explicitly. The issues of Islam and immigration are in fact on everyone's minds, and loom especially large in European public opinion, but are excluded from the official debate.

Unlike the situation in respect of NATO membership, the request for admission to the European Union poses a certain number of problems. In Europe there is first of all (and perhaps above all) a deep-seated reluctance on the part of Christian Democratic milieux and the centre-right in general to accept a Muslim country into what appears to be a 'Christian club'. (In 2002 the German Christian Democrats, as well as Valéry Giscard d'Estaing, said in so many words what many people think in secret.) There is also a fear of massive immigration, given that Turkey is experiencing a two-speed development that has made little impact on the southeastern regions. Finally, no one in Europe wishes the European Union to have a real border with the Middle East, where it might find itself embroiled, by means of an intermediary member state, in direct and conflictual relations with Syria, Iraq or Iran. The 'de-Middle Easternisation' of Turkey is perceived as a necessary condition if Turkey is to enter Europe.

On the Turkish side there are also signs of reluctance among nationalist and military circles, who hesitate to give in on the institutional demands (role of the army), the Kurdish question, and Cyprus (the army refused the proposal made by Kofi Annan in 2003). At the Copenhagen summit in December 2002, the European Union agreed to Cyprus's entry with or without an agreement between Turks and Greeks, thus placing Turkey on the defensive.

A TURKEY THAT IS MORE AND MORE EUROPEAN

Paradoxically, the victory of AK – a moderate Islamist party – has smoothed the path of Turkey toward Europe. First, there seems no longer to be an Islamist bogeyman: if in relation to contentious topics the ex-Islamists behave more moderately and in a more European fashion when in power than their social-democratic predecessors (like Ecevit), then there is no longer any stumbling-block to be found within Turkey. Moreover, AK sees the European demands for democratisation, respect for human rights and state reform as an echo of its own struggle against the army and the Islamists over the past 20 years. It is therefore in its best interests to play the European card. During the US-led campaign in Iraq (2003), Turkey (its government, Parliament, and public opinion) reacted like certain European countries, refusing to support US intervention. The reluctance of Turkey to act in the Middle East other than with regard to the Kurdish question brings it into line with European positions.

As for Islam, the fact that Europe sees itself increasingly as multi-religious (with official recognition in many countries of the Muslim presence) helps to bridge the gulf between a Turkey that is more lay than Muslim, that forbids the wearing of the veil in all institutional places, and a country like the Great Britain, which permits the veil in schools, in Parliament, and in the police force. Today the fundamental debate is not between Turkey and Europe, but concerns rather the very nature of Europe itself. A 'multi-speed' Europe, as Britain and Poland conceive of it, would be able to accommodate a nationalist Turkey, whereas a Europe moving towards greater integration would necessarily demand that Turkey call Kemalism into question.

It is therefore up to Europeans to agree on a definition of Europe. The debate surrounding Turkey's admission makes an essential contribution to that process.

TURKEY – A DEMOCRACY UNDER CONTROL?

The Turkish political system may usefully be described as that of a 'security regime', a concept according to which national security and the institutions of security play a pre-eminent role in the workings of the regime. The genesis of the security regime system dates back to the military coup of 12 September 1980, which defined the political equilibrium on which Turkey to some extent still depends today. The acknowledged goal of the military leaders at the time was to depoliticise society in order to put an end to the confrontations between different parties – leading to thousands of deaths at the end of the 1970s – and to eradicate the left by promoting a Turkish-Islamist ideology. The threat of the internal enemy made it possible to criminalize the opponents of the regime, and to legitimize violations of the rule of law by a prolonged period of exceptional state powers. Such institutional operation in the 1980s and 1990s, taking the reassuring form of a parliamentary system, in effect gave its blessing to the pervasive influence of the army.

FORMS OF THE PARLIAMENTARY SYSTEM

The first Turkish constitution dates from 1876, during the period of the *Tanzimat*. The republic was to have three more constitutions – the first in 1924, the second after the 'progressive' military coup in 1960, and the last one following that of 1980. On 12 September 1980, the National Security Council, dominated by the military, effectively dissolved Parliament and put in place a military administration that would last until the elections in spring 1983, made possible by the new constitution adopted on 7 November 1982.

The 1982 constitution, still in force but significantly amended over the past 20 years, recognizes the classic separation of powers and the sovereignty of Parliament. The legislative powers belong to the Turkish Grand National Assembly (*Türkiye Büyük Millet Meclisi*) made up of 550 deputies. Elections are held every five years, unless the body is dissolved by the President or by an act of Parliament. In practice, however, no legislature has ever served its full term. The deputies, moreover, enjoy an immunity that may be lifted by Parliament itself.

Executive power rests concurrently with the President and the government. The election of the President, who holds a non-renewable mandate of seven years, requires a majority of two-thirds of the members of Parliament. The President, whose role is normally that of an arbitrator – in the tradition of the French Fourth Republic – does not necessarily come from among the elected politicians. The current president, Ahmet Sezer, for example, is a former judge and thus initially an outsider to the world of politics.

Beyond the general role of representing the country as Head of State, the President convokes Parliament and promulgates the laws, although he may send some of them back to Parliament if he judges it necessary. Any law he deems to be in contravention of fundamental principles he may submit to the Constitutional Court, the members of which he appoints. The President also appoints the Prime Minister from among the members of Parliament, as well as the ministers, who are not necessarily elected deputies. After the government has been formed, it appears before Parliament for a vote of confidence on its programme, and thereafter takes responsibility for the political life of the country.

Such a brief description of a classic parliamentary system does not fully describe the reality of power in Turkey during the 1980s and 1990s. In fact, the army continued to exert a decisive influence until the elections of 2002. As recently as

1997, the coalition government dominated by the Refah, an Islamist party, was forced by the army to resign. The party was subsequently banned following a fervent campaign against 'the forces of reaction', and several of its leaders were imprisoned, including Erdogan, the Prime Minister. Moreover, the war against the PKK in the southeast has revealed the considerable autonomy exercised by the security forces, especially during the early 1990s when the Parliament had no control over their activities and the government itself had hardly any more authority over them.

THE ARMY

The internal workings of the army explain its capacity to impose its will in the political process. The military institutions used every measure at their disposal to present a united front in relation to the rest of society to ensure their independence from the political authorities. The ideological and social homogeneity of the military staff is assured by the rigour of the recruitment process and by regular purges. The army enquires into the family background – at least as far back as the grandparents – and the social relations of all candidates for the officers' training college. According to an enquiry in the late 1980s, a considerable percentage of officers (about 45 per cent) were recruited from among the sons of civil servants. The same source revealed that 11 per cent of the officers came from military families, 15 per cent from a working-class/labouring background (although the figure rises to 33 per cent if grandfathers are taken into account), 34 per cent from families of state employees, and 13 per cent from families of self-employed people. In addition, it seems that the social circles of Turkish military men were often limited to other civil servants or soldiers.

It would also appear that Kurds are greatly under-represented among the officer corps.

As a result, the hierarchy has largely been able to ensure that there is no political deviation, for the promotion of officers is controlled by the YAS (*Yüksek Askari Sura*, Superior

Military Council), which rejects a hundred or so cases each year. The decision of the authorities is political (no violation of regulations is necessary) and bears no appeal. An officer might thus be turned away because his wife wears the veil. Moreover, the army successfully rebutted a proposal that the schools of preaching imams might afford access to the competition for admission among the officer corps.

Although on the whole Turkish civil servants are rather poorly paid, the military is an exception, and the army has built up its own economic empire. Since the 1960s the army has taken control of a network of businesses not specifically connected to military activities (banking, cars, etc.) and has also remained the top land-owner in the country. This explains in part the army's current reticence with respect to certain privatisation schemes, and more generally, to an economic rationalization that would jeopardize its more diverse interests.

In addition to their salaries, soldiers enjoy numerous privileges and benefits, and the multiplication of guild-like 'foundations' (*vakif*) has made it possible to create an important social economy. For example, a *Mehmetçik Vakif* (military foundation) was created in July 1982 to help families of soldiers killed in combat. Finally, the return of former officers to the university or to the private sector helps consolidate the influence of the institution.

The strong position of the army within the political system has also enabled the Turkish army – unlike the armies of other NATO countries – to exclude any cut to its budget. The military budget in practice does not come under Parliament's control, and until 1999 the cost of the war against the PKK was so great – 10 billion dollars a year – that one could justifiably speak of a war economy. Defence spending apparently still represents one-third of the budget, and despite the state of its public finances, Turkey remains one of the top buyers worldwide of military equipment.

Teaching in the officers' schools puts the emphasis on the duty of defending Kemalist values, and clearly anticipates an intervention in the political sphere if and when the military establishment judges that national unity or the principle of secularity are under threat. In addition, unlike in Latin America, the army in Turkey does not generally identify with a social group but with the state, and as a result enjoys popular confidence, as has been borne out by the opinion polls.

THE NATIONAL SECURITY COUNCIL (MKG): A PARALLEL GOVERNMENT?

The three military coups d'état since the institution of the multiparty system have shown a growing involvement of the military establishment in the world of politics. The first coup was carried out outside the hierarchy, which was not to be the case subsequently – the last two revealed great cohesion within the military. Recently, however, the army has had to renounce any direct control over the government, because such control would have placed Turkey definitively beyond the pale as far as the European Union is concerned. Initially sporadic, the army's intervention has nonetheless become more regular. The generals openly express their views on public affairs, and at times contradict the government of the day. For example, the declaration by Prime Minister Erdogan of the need for political change in Cyprus was the object of immediate and vehement criticism by the military top brass.

At the institutional level, the Turkish army has afforded the MGK (*Milli Güvenlik Kurulu*, National Security Council) special privileges in order to ensure that they retain control. This Council was established by article 118 of the constitution of 1961 and is an institution, *de facto* in the hands of the army, that includes the President, the Prime Minister, a few ministers, the principal members of the officer corps, and the director of the MIT (*Milli Istihbarat Teskilati*, National Intelligence Organisation). The Secretary-General is a military man appointed by the chief of staff, and the decisions of the MGK, sometimes secret, are not subject to appeal.

Such secret arrangements empowering the MGK, revealed by the press in the summer of 2003 at the time of the institution's reform, suggest that the MGK functioned for 20 years as something like a parallel government. The MGK can 'advise' the government on all matters – foreign policy, privatisation, or the war on crime. Thus the decision to take action against the Islamists was passed by a resolution of the MGK dated 28 February 1997 concerning educational reform and the struggle against 'the forces of reaction' (*irtica*).

In addition to its widespread power, the MGK also has an important secretariat – staffed by military personnel – and is able to work directly with the principal administrations in order to verify that the measures adopted in the Council are being applied. The MGK intervenes, for example, in the National Planning Office (DPT), which is in charge of major infrastructure projects. Moreover, its status gives it the authority to launch 'psychological operations' aimed at manipulating public opinion and discrediting the opposition (Direction of Public Relations). The MGK also has the right to oversee the state television (TRT) and the semi-official Anatolia News Agency.

THE JUDICIARY IN POLITICAL LIFE

Control over the political field is also exercised by the country's judges. Indeed, Turkey is characterized by the significant influence of the judiciary in political life: political parties are frequently banned and candidates declared ineligible, which leads to serious legal battles with leftists, Islamists and Kurdish nationalists. To understand the legal reasoning behind such restrictions and bans, we must return to the interpretation of Turkish nationalism by the Constitutional Court, which alone has the power to issue bans on political parties.

First of all, the constitution of 1982 provided that 'no protection will be afforded to ideas and opinions contrary to Turkish national interests, to the principle of the indivisibility of the Turkish state and territory, or to Turkish moral and historical values.' Such a limited concept of freedom of thought and of speech serves to justify judicial procedures against the parties that run counter to constitutional principles.

In practice, nationalism and Kemalism – which are given the value of an immutable constitutional principle, since it is unthinkable to propose that they be modified by amendment – are defined in such a way that they exclude many important currents of thought from the legitimate political sphere. The Turkish Constitutional Court defined nationalism as distinct from a 'German' concept (based on heredity) – which has the support of nationalists of the extreme right – basing it instead on the notion of adherence to a political project and a common culture. The Court does not recognize the existence of the Kurdish minority, for the term 'minority' is reserved to communities mentioned in the Treaty of Lausanne of 1923 (Christians, essentially), and allows for neither discrimination against nor special status for citizens 'of Kurdish origin'.

This unitary concept of the republic *a priori* rules out a federal system, not to mention any right to self-determination. In practice, this line of argument served regularly to close down Kurdish nationalist parties in the 1990s. The Marxist movements were likewise considered to be unconstitutional, insofar as they called for the domination of one class by another, thus undermining national unity. Finally, the Islamists, by putting the religious bond – that of the community of believers – ahead of the national one, came equally under legal censure.

As a result of these measures, 23 parties have been banned by judicial decision since 1983. In addition, numerous leaders are regularly ruled ineligible by the YSK (Superior Electoral Council). Erdogan, the current Prime Minister, Erbakan, the renowned Islamist leader, and numerous militants on the left have been victims of such judgments. All have been condemned by the State Security Court under article 8 of the Anti-Terrorism Law and article 312 of the penal code. Yet Erdogan was able to get elected at a by-election after his party had received a majority in Parliament in November 2002, and succeeded in bringing in constitutional reform.

THE PARTIES

The MGK's control over the government does not extend to the whole of political life, which remains competitive and partly autonomous. After the 1980 coup d'état, the military failed to impose its candidates in the political arena, even though the generals, under Kenan Evren, had dissolved all parties (for the first time in Turkey's modern history), banned the principal political leaders from public office for five to ten years, and eliminated on average 20 per cent of the candidates for election in 1983.

Even if it is clear that there was popular support for the intervention of the generals, the voters never ratified the army's choices, and the victory of Özal in 1983 was neither foreseen nor desired by General Evren. Such resistance by the voters was not a new phenomenon, however. In 1961 the army supported the CHP (or PRP, Republican People's Party), but it was the Adalet Partisi (a conservative party and successor to the Demokrat Partisi) that won the election. Likewise in 1971, the military supported the centre parties and yet it was the PRP that gained the majority in the 1973 elections. Occasionally, politicians have succeeded in forcing the hand of the army – notably by decreeing an amnesty for all the leaders banned from political activity after the 1980 coup. Political life thus enjoys a certain autonomy that the military is obliged to take into account, and that makes for the distinctive sorts of tensions that exist within the security regime.

This situation has generally posed no threat to the control exercised by the military, apart from the period when the ANAP, under the presidency of Turgut Özal (1989–93), had insufficient power to resist them on certain policy issues. The ongoing fragmentation that the political sphere has been undergoing since the early 1990s explains the succession of incohesive and short-lived governments (a year on average). The pressure of the army on a party – for instance in 1997 – never brought with it any reaction of solidarity by the political class that had come to accept their role in political activity.

Moreover, the political parties are generally organisations whose heads control the resources and behave in an autocratic manner. For several years now, all opinion surveys have shown that there is very low confidence in the political parties. Government instability and repeated scandals explain the unprecedented volatility of the electorate, and a growing abstention rate. The DSP, which obtained 22 per cent of the votes in 1999, collapsed in 2002 with only 1.23 per cent of the votes. Under these conditions the credibility of the parties is limited. The politicians, especially the elected deputies, do not enjoy sufficient popularity to resist the pressures of the army.

PARLIAMENT

The influence of the Grand National Assembly is limited by a series of constraints. In the first place, the current electoral system has the effect of restricting its representative nature. For according to the current rules, parties who receive less than 10 per cent of the votes at the national level have no representation in Parliament. This measure, intended to prevent fragmentation of the political landscape, has been a failure: the number of parties competing during elections tends to increase. As a result, after the elections of 3 November 2002, less than half of the voters were represented in Parliament, where only two parties – CHP and AK – were present.

Furthermore, the weak ideological commitment of many deputies means that changes in party affiliation are frequent. Parties that are losing ground see their deputies rally to a more successful rival. The DSP was thus reduced from 156 to 58 elected members before the elections of 2002. It is therefore not surprising that among the deputies of the AKP there are a not insignificant number of defectors from other parties. Members of Parliament are rarely re-elected, apart from a few prominent politicians whose position is well established. Newcomers in general amount to over 50 per cent, and peaked at 80 per cent during the parliamentary elections of 2002.

As a result, a political career is often reduced to a fairly brief stint in the Assembly, and there is a temptation accordingly to try to benefit from such a temporary position through illegal means. In the late 1980s 104 deputies were under investigation (at the parliamentary stage) for different reasons, from assassination to misappropriation of funds. Since November 2002, 88 deputies who have not been re-elected, and thus no longer enjoy immunity, were the subjects of legal action. Parliament has for the most part been reluctant to lift the immunity of deputies, with the exception of Kurdish nationalist members, a group of whom were as a result condemned in the 1990s to long prison sentences.

Parliament enacts laws, but its initiatives are in part under the control of the President and the Constitutional Court. The AKP government currently in power has over the past year run the gamut of the various institutions for resisting proposed reforms. President Ahmet Sezer, who succeeded Süleyman Demirel in 2000, opted for an interventionist policy and on several occasions returned bills to Parliament. Unlike Demirel, who tended to protect the consensus among the parties and was sensitive to the opinion of the military, Sezer has a less consensual approach to his role, and has not hesitated overtly to oppose certain legislative measures of the Ecevit government, and even more often those of Erdogan. His opposition to the bill proposing to allow US troops to cross Turkish soil in order to invade Iraq, which Parliament in the end rejected, indicates a presidency that is concerned with international law but which often behaves as a political adversary of the government.

INSTITUTIONAL REFORM

The pace of reform of the Turkish political system has considerably accelerated as a result of the conjunction of three elements.

First, Turkey's major national non-political institutions have since the end of the 1980s been in favour of political normalisation in order to rationalize the workings of the state, notably by diminishing military expenditures and ensuring a place for Turkey in the European Union.

Secondly, the EU has a considerable effect on the internal political equilibrium of Turkey. The majority of legislation passed in the last few years has been undertaken in the spirit of bringing Turkey into conformity with the Union. This theme was central during the early elections of 2002, in particular because of the economic crisis that hit the country severely. Yet inclusion within the EU presupposes a rupture in the current political and institutional equilibrium. The European Commission has for instance indicated on several occasions that the excessive weight of the military presence presents a major obstacle to fulfilling the criteria articulated at the Copenhagen summit.

Finally, the vote of 3 November 2002, reflecting the dissatisfaction of the electorate with the incumbents, made it possible for a single-party government to come to power, the first since the end of the 1980s, with a sufficient majority to carry out institutional reform. (Constitutional reforms must be accepted by three-fifths of the deputies, after having been proposed by one-third of them.)

The MGK saw its role considerably modified in the summer of 2003. Its Secretary-General is henceforth a civilian, the meetings – which used to be monthly – are now bi-monthly, and the deputy Prime Minister and the Minister of Justice have become members of the MGK, thus reinforcing the number of civilians in relation to military members. Its decisions are no longer binding on the government. Legally, of course, they never were mandatory, but the principle has been reaffirmed and the power relations are now more favourable to the civilian members. Certain generals, notably the last military Secretary-General of the MGK, Tuncer Kilinc, severely criticised these measures, which he claimed run the risk of weakening national security. If the government can hope gradually to free itself from the power of the generals, civilian control of the military is an objective that will be difficult to realize in the short term.

The military institution remains *de facto* autonomous, and the Minister of Defence has no say in appointments to or the general orientation of his ministry.

A favourable conjunction of factors thus makes it possible to foresee an end to the security regime set up following the coup d'état of 1980, but the first efforts in this direction under Özal showed how difficult the process would be and how unsure its results, for it goes to the heart of political practices and interests that are deeply rooted.

THE TURKISH ECONOMY BETWEEN NEO-LIBERALISM AND THE DOMINANCE OF STATISM

Turkey, whose national product was over US $200 billion in 2003, constitutes an important regional economic power and represents a relatively open market of about 70 million inhabitants. The only country to have entered into a customs union with the European Union without being a member, Turkey's economy is gradually being integrated into the single market after having accepted terms and conditions for entry into the Community at the end of 1999. The country also remains a regional production and export centre. Yet the per capita national product remains low – between $2,500 and $3,000 – and the per capita GDP in terms of purchasing power in 2002 was 25 per cent of the European average (according to figures provided by the Turkish National Institute of Statistics, Devlet Istatistik Enstitusu). Macroeconomic instability and the unpredictable nature of the economy – largely the result of strong, endemic inflation – constitute the principal obstacles to the full realization of the country's development potential and expose it to recurrent crises.

The state-directed, protectionist model of development elaborated in the 1930s made it possible to lay the foundations for Turkey's industrialization. Since that time, the policy of economic liberalization and of opening up to the rest of the world undertaken in the 1980s and pursued via the creation of a customs union with the EU, has led to the development of the private sector, in which small and medium-sized enterprises (SMEs) constitute the central pillar of the economy. Exports, predominantly aimed at the EU, Turkey's main trading partner, became the motor of economic growth.

Nevertheless, the weight of the state has continued to make itself felt in the core industries and in the banking sector. Thus the struggle against inflation and the stabilization of the financial sector has taken the form of disengagement by the state and reinforcement of the institutional framework necessary for a smoother functioning of the market economy.

A STATE-CONTROLLED AND PROTECTIONIST MODEL OF DEVELOPMENT

In the early 1930s, in an increasingly protectionist international environment, the Turkish government adopted a policy of industrialization that gave primacy to the state. There was scepticism about private initiative in economic matters fuelled by the desire to avoid a dispersion of political power: the unity of the Turkish nation-state required a centralization at both the political and the economic levels. As a result, the state became the principal economic actor – its control was exercised through state-owned enterprises, which were strongly represented in the agrarian sector, transportation and communications.

In 1940, the national protection law allowed the government to exert even closer control over the national economy – so much so that in the 1950s, public enterprises were responsible for over half of the industrial production in the country. This commercial regime served the logic of statist development. The state, by controlling imports, regulated the activity of the Turkish private sector. Moreover, protectionism was intended to shield the nascent national industry from international competition and to defend the value of the national currency.

The dominant role of the state in the 1930s was not fundamentally challenged until the early 1980s, for the state enterprises were seen as the legacy of the founder of the Turkish republic, Mustafa Kemal, whereas an attitude of suspicion towards international trade remained firmly rooted in the mentality. In addition, towards the late 1970s the percentage of exports in Turkey's GNP did not exceed 5 per cent, while the quantity of imports remained negligible. Measures taken to stabilize the economy during times of crisis were aimed solely at adjusting foreign trade and the balance of payments: the logic underlying the strategy of growth by replacing imports with domestic goods was never called into question until the 1980s.

THE TURNING-POINT OF THE 1980s: OPENING UP TO THE OUTSIDE WORLD

The increase in exports during the 1980s was the fruit of a policy of promoting exports that relied on three pillars: the exchange rate policy, the credit-granting policy, and fiscal subsidies. The lowering of protective tariffs began in 1984, with a 20 per cent reduction in customs duties. A few years later the maximum customs duty was set at 50 per cent. However, this liberalization was accompanied by the introduction of supplementary charges for the exporter, among which were municipal taxes for transportation and the use of infrastructure, fiscal stamps, the financing of supporting funds and price controls, and expenditure on improving housing. The difficulties involved in this policy of subsidies prompted the government to put an end to it in 1988. At the same time, quantitative restrictions on imports were eliminated and, from the early 1990s, the liberalization of the commercial system picked up speed. From then on, no prior authorization was required for importing goods.

The policy of economic liberalization in the 1980s gradually called into question an approach to development that was traditionally directed by the public authorities, and in which the state and publicly-owned enterprises exercised a strong influence especially on the core industries and the banking sector. A wave of privatisations began in the early 1980s as a result of the policy of economic liberalization. Unfortunately, the total income from privatisation remained fairly modest: since 1985 it has represented only 5 per cent of GDP. The Turkish economy has therefore to rely on other assets, and in particular on the vitality of its SMEs.

SMEs, BACKBONE OF THE TURKISH ECONOMY

Turkey currently has a diversified economy dominated by the tertiary sector, of which services constitute 60 per cent of national production. Although great social and regional disparities remain, with an industrial sector centred largely in the Marmara region, the process of economic liberalization begun in the 1980s allowed Turkey to develop a dynamic class of private entrepreneurs. Thus the private sector is the source of 80 per cent of value-added. Although there are large public enterprises and companies engaged in the export trade, businesses with fewer than 250 employees form the cornerstone of the Turkish economy. As a result, the output of SMEs represents 30 per cent of the value-added in the manufacturing industry, and 60 per cent of jobs in the sector, half of the manufacturing industry being concentrated in micro-enterprises with fewer than ten employees.

These companies – for the most part family businesses – serve as shock absorbers, for they have a great capacity for adapting to developments in the commercial environment. They nevertheless suffer from limited access to credit, since the private sector is still neglected in favour of the financing needs of the public sector. Furthermore, the proportion of investments in the former sector remains low. In 1997 it represented 26.4 per cent of GDP, and in 2001 17.8 per cent of GDP. Yet the expansion of the tertiary sector has been accompanied by a decline of the primary sector.

The Primary Sector

Between 1997 and 2001, the contribution of agriculture to the gross value-added dropped from 13.8 per cent to 12.1 per cent. Employment in the same sector declined from 40.8 per cent in 1997 to 35.4 per cent in 2001. Meanwhile, in the service sector it rose from 35.1 per cent to 41 per cent between 1997 and 2001. Nevertheless, in spite of this significant decline agriculture continues to play a major role as a sector to which jobless people turn in times of crisis.

The new agricultural policy adopted in 2000 initiated an ambitious reform programme that has been carried out with the aid of the World Bank. Turkey opted for a system of direct aid to farmers, gradually eliminating the system of credit and subsidies to those entering the sector. The reform provided also for the reconversion of tobacco, tea, and nut growing. State subsidies to agriculture and rural development represented a total of about 1.3 per cent of the state budget in 2002. The modernization of Turkish agriculture can serve as the basis for the introduction of the European Common Agricultural Policy (CAP). It must, however, be supplemented by an improvement in the structures and modernisation of production methods.

Nevertheless, agricultural trade between Turkey and its primary commercial partner, the European Union, remains weak. In 2002 Turkish exports to the EU, essentially consisting of fruits and vegetables, were worth around 2 million euros. Exports of cereals, oleaginous grains and dairy products from the EU represented 1 million euros. The vitality of the Turkish economy thus comes not from agriculture but from elsewhere – namely the automobile and the textile and clothing industries.

The Automotive Sector

In Turkey, the automotive sector is dominated largely by foreign manufacturers, 90 per cent of which are European. Developments between 1992 and 2000 reveal the growing importance to the EU of Turkey's foreign trade. In 1992, 35 per cent of Turkey's trade in motor vehicles and 78 per cent of its spare parts were with the EU and the European Free Trade Association (EFTA). In 2000 the proportion was 81 per cent and 69 per cent respectively.

The customs union has been the key factor in implementing the new export-oriented production strategy. Certain car manufacturers such as Renault and Fiat, whose operations in Turkey were set up in the 1970s, had to modify their strategy and make Turkey into an international production site.

Renault thus decided to stop production of the R9, R12, and R19 in order to concentrate on making modern cars largely for an export market, such as the Mégane Classique and Tourer from 1999, and then the Clio Symbol (known in Turkey and France as the Tricorps). The Renault factory in Bursa became the only plant in the world producing the Mégane Tourer for export to Western Europe. The Clio, on the other hand, is exported to North Africa, the CEEC (Central and Eastern European Countries) and Russia. In September 2003 Renault launched mass production at its Bursa plant of the new four-door Mégane.

Yet these strategies on the part of Renault and Ford – to name only the most active companies – mean the transfer of certain production units from the EU to Turkey. For Turkey offers a number of advantages: its labour force is qualified and cheaper, the existing infrastructures make possible the development of a modern industry, and the fiscal situation is favourable – no tax is levied on vehicles exported from Turkey. But even though the automotive sector is experiencing significant growth, it is textiles and clothing that remain the prime source of Turkey's exports: it relies on a national industry that is able to profit from its competitive advantage.

The Textile and Clothing Sector

The textile and clothing sector represents 40 per cent of industrial jobs, thus carrying considerable weight in the Turkish economy. It represents 8 per cent of national production (12.5 per cent of total industrial production). In the 1980s, the textile sector's share of the country's export trade grew steadily until it reached 50 per cent in the 1990s. From 1987 onwards, Turkey, which exported primarily textiles, began to turn its attention to exporting articles of clothing. And so whereas the volume of clothing exported by Turkey in 1980 was valued at $700 million, by 1997 it had risen to $9.8 billion.

At the international level, in 1997 Turkey's share of global exports of textiles and clothing was 4 per cent. The sector has remained the country's leading export field, representing a third of all exports. On the basis of these figures Turkey in that year ranked ninth in the world after China, the United States, India, Pakistan, Taiwan, Brazil, South Korea and Indonesia, and exported to 150 countries. Moreover, Turkey ranked sixth among world producers of cotton after China, the United States, India, Pakistan, and Uzbekistan. The European market continues to absorb two-thirds of Turkey's textile and clothing exports. With an 11.4 per cent market share, Turkey represents the second largest supplier to the European Union after China (14.7 per cent) but ahead of Hong Kong (8.4 per cent). It is only in the German market that Turkey comes ahead of China.

Furthermore, if we move beyond the borders of the European Union, the situation is much the same. Turkey is far ahead of Tunisia, Romania and Morocco. Total industrial production in the countries that make up the CEEC and the countries south of the Mediterranean amounts to 50.1 billion euros, of which Turkey alone accounts for 30.2 billion.

The Turkish textile and clothing industry is distinct from that of the European periphery, for unlike the CEEC and the Mediterranean countries, which suffer from the narrow range of their industrial fabrics, Turkey has a complete range of high-quality products. The vitality of the local textile industry has made co-contracting possible. Moreover, the creativity of Turkish industry is significant, for 10 per cent of Turkish exports are of domestic brands. In this domain Turkey has been able to take advantage of the vitality of its international trade.

TRADE WITH EUROPE AND THE REST OF THE WORLD

Turkey remains the only non-member state that has a customs union with the EU. This was the result of decision 1/95 adopted by the Association Council in December 1995, creating a customs union between the European Community and Turkey that would come to define the commercial policy of the country. It applies to most goods and merchandise, with the notable exception of agricultural products. This decision constituted a fundamental step in the process of liberalization of Turkey's trade: free trade within the territory covered by the customs union and the adoption of a common commercial policy greatly increased the openness of the Turkish economy. Turkey was obliged to align itself with the common tariff applied by the EU to non-member states. Since 1 January 2001, Turkey has applied the same duties to products covered by 1/95 coming from third-party countries as does the European Union.

In 1995, on the eve of the creation of the customs union, the volume of trade between Turkey and the EU amounted to only $28.9 billion. Six years later, it had reached $34.4 billion. The volume of exports from Turkey rose from $11 billion in 1995 to $16 billion in 2001. Imports from the EU went from $16.8 billion to $26.6 billion in 2000, and then to $18 billion in 2001. It is worth noting that between 1995 and 2000 the EU's imports from third-party countries declined by 19 per cent, while Turkey's market share of total EU imports remained constant at 1.7 per cent. In 2003, the EU was thus Turkey's most important commercial partner, even if the customs union has not substantially altered their relations. In 2002, 52.2 per cent of Turkish exports were destined for EU countries and 48.1 per cent of imports came from the Community. The following year half of Turkish exports were to the EU, while Turkey continued to buy a little under half of its imports from member states.

Germany is Turkey's principal trading partner. In 2001, 33.3 per cent of Turkish exports were to Germany, and German goods represented 29.2 per cent of all Turkey's imports. Italy is its second largest trading partner: its share of Turkey's exports and imports amounts to 14.5 per cent and 19 per cent respectively. Nevertheless, despite some good results, the Turkish economy remains very fragile and vulnerable to crises.

INFLATION AND PUBLIC FINANCE

The Turkish economy has been characterized by successive periods of short-term rapid growth and endemic inflation, which prevents the economy from realizing its potential for long-term growth. A high inflation rate, even when it is foreseeable, brings with it not insignificant costs, of which the most important is the absence of perspective beyond the short-term, resulting in considerable distortions of profit margins and exacerbating the inequality of revenues that is characteristic of the Turkish economy.

At the end of 1999, Turkey launched an ambitious programme of stabilization, intended to bring the inflation rate below 10 per cent by 2002. This programme rests on three essential pillars: a firm monetary and exchange-rate policy, restructuring public finances in order to eliminate the principal source of inflationary tensions, and launching widespread structural reforms liberalizing and modernising the economy. In 2000 and at the beginning of 2001, this anti-inflationary programme reduced the inflation rate in consumer prices over 12 months from 69 per cent in 1999 to 33 per cent in February 2001. But political tensions and the tight money market subjected the Turkish financial market to serious difficulties, leading to a financial crisis in February 2001. The programme that had begun in December 1999 ended in failure, notably on account of the fragility of the Turkish banking sector and a loss of credibility due to the rapid rise of external imbalances and the tight financial markets. The announcement of a conflict at the upper echelons of the state precipitated a flight of $7.5 billion from the country on the eve of an important Treasury auction. The government was obliged to allow the lira to float, putting an end to the policy of an adjustable pegged exchange rate indexed to a dollar/euro basket according to a target inflation rate. Between February and December 2001 the Turkish lira fell by 50 per cent in relation to the dollar.

This devaluation led to a sudden rise in prices – an increase of 68.5 per cent in the consumer price index in 2001, a 14 per cent fall in demand, a decline of 10 per cent in volume of private consumption, and a fall of 30 per cent in investments made by enterprises. The GNP contracted by 9.5 per cent, making 2001 the worst year of recession in the country since World War II.

The fundamental cause of this stubborn inflation, as well as of the irregular nature of growth in Turkey, is the persistence of high budget deficits. Financing these deficits through domestic borrowing compels the central bank to create liquidities, which promotes inflation. This financing also leads the banking system to grant credit, thus depriving the productive sector of capital. The gradual modification of Turkey's foreign borrowing capacity, as well as the high level of amortization needed because of the short maturity of the debt stock, have inevitably increased the Treasury's refinancing risk. This in turn has led to a rise in the rate of interest on the outstanding obligations. Furthermore, the seriousness of the budgetary problem has been exacerbated by the tightness of capital markets and by the pursuit of populist politics. The result has been the adoption of supplementary budgets, recourse to extra-budgetary funds, poor management of public enterprises, and deficits incurred by the social security organizations.

Between 1990 and 1999 the public debt ratio rose from 29 per cent to 61 per cent of GNP. The increase in domestic debt has been even more significant. In 1990 the ratio of domestic debt to GNP was 6 per cent. By 1999 it had risen to 42 per cent. Previous experience shows the need to act upon two levels: on the one hand, the budget must be tightened up, while at the same time the necessary structural reforms must be put through in order to remedy fundamental institutional weaknesses that contribute to inadequate control of deficits. For the budgetary excesses can be attributed in large part to the omnipresence of the state in the economy.

TOWARDS REDUCING THE PRESENCE OF THE STATE IN THE ECONOMY

The structural reforms aimed at reducing the presence of the state in the economy call for disengagement by the public authorities from the productive sector and the abandonment of subsidies, in order to allow market forces to determine the allocation of resources. The role of the state is moving towards that of a guarantor of conditions that are indispensable for a market economy. The economic programme presented in May 2001 enjoyed strong political support, and rested upon a fundamental policy of structural reforms. In 2002 Turkey concluded a stand-by agreement with the IMF, intended essentially to remedy the structural weaknesses of the Turkish economy and liberalize the agricultural and energy markets, as well as to combat political interventions that have been a source of economic instability. The results have begun to be felt. Budgetary discipline and transparency in public sector accounts have improved, inflationary pressure has diminished, and the Central Bank has become more independent.

At the present time, public enterprises represent around 5 per cent of GDP and 19 per cent of value-added in the manufacturing sector. The economic activities of the state are concentrated in a few key areas such as banking, energy, and basic industries. Although the state banks' share represents only 1 per cent of GDP, it accounts for one-third of value-added in the banking sector. The reform process intended to restructure and strengthen the sector has brought the management of the banks gradually in line with market conditions. The public enterprises have often been overstaffed and not very productive. Yet their products, the prices of which are not determined on the free market, are destined primarily for the manufacturing sector. Price distortions are thus multiplied through the whole economy.

The current economic policy is aimed at reducing the price distortions caused by the presence of the state in the production sector. In the agricultural sector the system of guaranteed prices has largely been eliminated, and the prices of tobacco and sugar are now determined by supply and demand rather than by state purchasing. A similar deregulation also applies to the energy sector – production and distribution of electricity have also been reorganized and are now overseen by an independent authority responsible for regulating the energy market. The natural gas sector has even been opened up to competition since November 2002.

Nevertheless, the public company Botas continues to engage in international trade, transport and warehousing, and thus remains the sole provider of gas on the Turkish market. However, creating independent bodies to regulate the market and monitor competition helps reinforce the role of market forces. Moreover, the legal framework for privatisations has been improved.

The Major Privatisations

An amendment of the constitution has made possible international arbitration in and privatisation of the energy sector. In 2002 the government's shares in the petrol distribution firm Poaş were sold, as were 31.5 per cent of the shares in the Tüpras petroleum refinery. The privatisation programme of 2003 included plans to sell some long-standing sectoral monopolies: 130 firms were included in this privatisation scheme, intended to generate revenues of $4 billion. The list of enterprises to be privatised includes the petrochemical companies Petkim and Petrokimya, the metallurgical firms Eti Silver and Eti Metallurgy, the Tüpras refinery, the Tekel cigarette and alcoholic drinks manufacturer, the telecommunications provider Türk Telekom, and Turkish Airlines. The banking sector has also been subject to numerous reforms.

Restructuring the Banking Sector

The financial sector, which is still in the process of being reorganized, does not put enough savings into productive investment. During the 1990s there was strong public demand for credit and a certain degree of laxity in regulating and monitoring the financial markets. This made possible the rapid development of the banking sector, which is dominated by three public banks that together hold 30 per cent of total assets. There are also several private banks owned by conglomerates of family enterprises. The process of reorganization has been accelerated since the financial crisis of February 2001. It seeks to restructure the financing profile of banks in difficulty, and to reinforce the financial foundations of the sector by bringing prudential regulations more rapidly in line with international norms. About 20 banks that have proved unviable, representing around 15 per cent of all assets, were placed under the control of the savings and deposit guarantee fund. Turkey can count on the internationalization of its economy to further strengthen this process.

Foreign Direct Investment

Annual foreign direct investment (FDI) in Turkey remains below 1 per cent of GDP, while the total amount of FDI represents only 9 per cent of GDP. This places considerable limitation upon the modernisation of capital. Over 98 per cent of foreign direct investment in Turkey comes from OECD countries, and over 85 per cent from European Union countries. Over the last five years, funds from FDI in the Turkish economy have financed 4 per cent of private fixed investments. The distribution of approved projects by sector indicates that 55 per cent of the funds go to manufacturing industries, and 40 per cent to the service sector. It is thus clear that total FDI over the past few years has remained weak in relation to the potential and size of a country such as Turkey. The major reasons for this are economic and political instability as well as the complexity and opacity of administrative procedures. The new framework law on foreign direct investments may, in this regard, prove to be a basis for liberalizing the Turkish economy.

The low amounts of FDI can be misleading with regard to the share of foreign capital in the Turkish economy. There are 125 enterprises with foreign participation among the 500 largest publicly-traded industrial companies, according to the figures for 2000. These firms represent total revenues of $15.5 billion, which is 28 per cent of the combined business revenues of the top 500 companies. Companies with foreign capital exported $4.4 billion-worth of goods in 2000, representing 17 per cent of total exports. Companies with foreign investment are numerous in automotive production, refineries and electrical supplies. In addition to industry, they also have a strong presence in distribution and insurance.But foreign investment can only grow in an economic environment that is more favourable towards investment in general.

A WAY OUT OF THE CRISIS?

Turkey has succeeded in taking advantage of its strategic importance to western countries in order to obtain massive financial aid from the IMF. An agreement involving $16 billion was signed in February 2002, of which $9 billion were made immediately available. The programme implemented by the Minister of the Economy, Kemal Dervis, former vice-president of the World Bank, and pursued vigorously by the AKP government during 2003, made it possible to stabilize the economy and accelerate structural reforms. The year 2002 saw inflation reduced to a historically low level for Turkey, accompanied by a return of growth. This movement was confirmed in 2003. Growth in 2002 was 7.8 per cent, and 5.8 per cent in the first half of 2004, while inflation fell to 28 per cent in 2003 as compared to 55 per cent the previous year.

Furthermore, the limited impact of the Iraq War on the economy in 2003 attests to the vigour of internal forces favouring growing market confidence, as well as to the country's capacity to withstand external shocks. By complying with the Community *acquis* (common terms and conditions for membership), Turkey has shown its ability to take the measures that follow from the first agreements signed with the EU. Nevertheless, only the pursuit of structural reforms, along with inflation control, will make it possible to bring about lasting economic stability and predictability. In a market economy, these two conditions constitute the condition *sine qua non* for a country to be able to realize its full development potential. This is the cost of ensuring that the viability of the Turkish economy and its capacity to confront competitive pressures are guaranteed once and for all in the event of its entry into the single market.

ISLAM IN TURKEY:
A 'SECULAR MUSLIM' STATE

On both sides of the Bosporus, the religious question is often at the core of the debates over the integration of Turkey into Europe. Domestically, it is common to vilify the reluctance of the Europeans and accuse the European Union of being a 'Christian club'. In the Europe of Fifteen and now of Twenty-Five, a significant part of public opinion has been wondering whether a Muslim country, even if officially secular, can ever claim to be European in character. Yet it is clear that one must move beyond speaking simply of 'Islam' – a term that is far too general, often reified and used with negative connotations – and focus instead on the specificities and the history of Islam in Turkey. Taking the latter approach will make it evident that relations between the state and religion, the diversity of Turkish Islam, as well as its social and political expressions are poorly understood. Greater familiarity with these facets of the country will make possible a re-evaluation of the question of its 'compatibility' with Europe.

AN AMBIGUOUS SECULARITY

Turkey is often represented as the only country that is at one and the same time both 'Muslim' and 'secular'. What a destiny for a country that is heir to the greatest Muslim empire in the world, one that dominated the Muslim and Arab world for six centuries! The Ottoman Empire was not only the centuries-old seat of the caliphate, but Islam was its state religion and the source of its legitimacy, no matter how multi-religious the Empire may have been. Thus the Ottoman rulers adopted the motto 'The sword of Islam and the shadow of God on earth', adapting perfectly the institutions of the Orthodox Christian patriarchate of Constantinople and giving rise to a hitherto unprecedented institutionalization of Islam at the heart of the state.

It was clearly in order to break with this tradition that Mustafa Kemal wished to found a secular republic based on a wholly different source of legitimacy. The Kemalist reforms, the aim of which was the long-term secularisation of society, made religion their chief target, rejecting the Arabic alphabet – considered by the republican elites to be a sign of backwardness – and changing the rhythms of life by replacing the Muslim calendar with the Gregorian. One of the ambitions of Kemalism was to create a new kind of Turkish citizen, free of all outward sign of his or her relationship to the Muslim community – relegated henceforth to the private sphere – and moving instead closer to Europe, the symbol of civilization.

At the institutional level, the republican government abolished the sultanate in 1922 and the caliphate in 1924; it closed the Qur'anic schools, thus putting an end to the training of new theologians. In 1926 Kemal replaced *sharia* as the source of law with an adapted version of the Swiss civil law code. In 1928 the abolition of Islam as the state religion brought an end to the religious legitimisation of its political order. And in 1937, as the final stage in the process of secularisation, the principle of secularity was written into the constitution.

Such a secularity of the state should, however, be qualified – relations between the Turkish state and religion are far from being as simple as might appear at first glance. In reality, Turkey has no true separation of religion and state. Immediately following the abolition of the caliphate on 3 March 1924, Mustafa Kemal created a Directorate of Religious Affairs, the *Diyanet İşleri Başkanliği* (DIB). Directly attached to the Prime Minister's cabinet, this institution is responsible for regulating and administering all matters of belief and liturgical rite. Since the early days of the Republic, the *Diyanet* has reserved a special place for religion, principally within the context of education and liturgical practice. As a result, courses in Qur'anic learning were never suspended: it is the *Diyanet* that trains the imams (turning religious leaders into state functionaries), controls the 'clergy', and determines the sermons that are to be read in the mosques on Fridays. It is also this body that organizes the pilgrimage to Mecca.

Far from having burned all bridges with religion, the 'secular' state thus continues to be responsible for its organization and teaching. The *Diyanet* symbolizes the ambiguity of creating such a grand religious apparatus to protect the constitutional principle of secularity. A simple office with a staff of several thousand at the time of its creation, this department has continued to grow ever since. In 1981 its budget was greater than that of the Ministry of Industry, and has not stopped increasing since that time, reaching about 400 million euros by 2002. At present the office manages more than 75,000 mosques, about 90,000 civil servants, and 75,000 employees. As a generator of religious norms that it seeks to impose on society, the Turkish state wants to retain exclusive control and ultimate authority over religious affairs.

Ironically, this practice is reminiscent of Ottoman tradition, for over the long term the Kemalist reforms appear indeed to be but one stage in the long process of the domestication of Islam by the state. As compared to the Ottoman era, the republican state has made an even stronger claim to a monopoly in matters of religion. The reason for this is, first of all, that non-Muslim religious groups, which were numerous under the Ottoman Empire and enjoyed considerable religious and legal autonomy under the *millet* system, are no longer present in significant numbers. Society has been made homogeneous in religious terms through the massacres of the Armenians in 1915, the exchange of Orthodox Christian populations of Turkey for the Muslims of Greece in 1922, the emigration of some Jews after the creation of the state of Israel, and the flight of the majority of Greeks from Istanbul to Greece following the violence of September 1955. The great majority of Turks, who today are 99% Muslim, are therefore subject to the *Diyanet*.

A second reason is that the state has sought to restrict all divergent expressions of Islam that might escape its control. Thus, for instance, Muslim brotherhoods have been banned and convents closed down since 1925. Finally, religious currents that were violently opposed in the early years of the republic have been pushed underground.

This domestication of religion did not prevent the Kemalist regime from instrumentalising Islam at the time of the transition from the Empire to the Republic, and using it generally to reaffirm national cohesion – the cohabitation of Kurds and Turks did, after all, require a minimum of common values. After the 1980 coup the Turkish army, while outlawing certain public references to Islam, once again favoured religion as a point of reference for national unity. From the perspective of nation-building, Islam has played the role of a *de facto* official religion and has been an important factor in defining national identity. Because religious practice today is very widespread, even republicans who are far from observant worshippers nonetheless consider themselves to be true Muslims. Just as in the days of the Empire, the *Diyanet* serves, paradoxically, to legitimise power, and in this capacity must implement a national version of Islam that claims to be enlightened and modern.

UNDER A FRAGILE UNITY, A DIVERSITY OF ISLAMS

But what sort of Islam are we talking about? In keeping with the project of creating a unitary national community and rejecting any particularistic elements, Kemalism ignores all religious diversity, although there is very real diversity in Turkey today. In practice, if Kemalism often turned to religious references as sources of its legitimization, it was always to Hanafite Sunnism that it appealed – that is, to an Islam that is quite orthodox and traditionalist – thereby making it the official branch of Islam by default. Hanafite Sunnism is one of the four great schools of Islamic law, tracing its origins to the work of Abu Hanifah (d. 150 AH). 'Secularism' thus does not mean the recognition of religious equality or even pluralism, but on the contrary affords official status to the Hanafite Sunni school.

What does the – largely unknown – pluralism of Turkish Islam consist of? If we confine ourselves to Sunni Islam, the Hanafite school is the predominant one, even though the Kurds, who are also principally Sunnis, are mainly Shafite. But Turkish Islam is above all divided along the denominational split between Sunnis and Alevis.

The Alevis are a heterodox, syncretistic group that makes up the hidden face, as it were, of Turkish Islam. Although the group represents a not insignificant proportion of the country's population – between 10 per cent and 25 per cent according to some estimates – it remains all the more difficult to identify because the unitary policy of Turkey renders it statistically invisible. The group shares some similarities with others scattered over a territory stretching from the Balkans (the Kizilbash of Bulgaria, the Bektashis of Albania) to Iran (*Ahl-i haqq*) by way of Syria (the Alawites). On account of certain elements of Shi'a origin in their worship (the veneration of Ali, fasting during the month of Muharrem, etc.), the Alevis are sometimes considered 'extremist Shiites'. But in reality they follow an esoteric interpretation of Islam and are distinguished by certain very distinctive elements (ceremonies, or *cem*; holy men, or *dede*; the cult of stones, etc.) the precise origins of which are difficult to determine, and some of which probably predate Islam.

There is great diversity among Alevis, both in linguistic terms – in addition to a Turkish-speaking majority there are significant groups that speak Kurdish, Zaza, or Arabic – and with respect to worship and even individual matters of faith. This makes it all the more difficult to classify them. As a result, the attitude of orthodox Muslims towards the Alevis oscillates between denying that they are genuinely Muslim or assimilating them to orthodox Islam by denying their specificity, and, at the other extreme, considering their distinctive elements to be 'deviations' that are now obsolete. The authorities – for whom Alevism represents at most a cultural phenomenon – deny its specificity or treat it as a form of folklore.

But sectarian diversity is not the only distinctive feature of Turkish Islam. In their relationship to Islam, Turks in a sense represent a 'cultural exception' by virtue of the survival of pre-Islamic elements that continue to manifest themselves in the form of popular religion. For instance, visits to *ziyaret* (pilgrimage sites, often mausoleums) in search of cures for certain illnesses are widely undertaken, despite being frequently denounced for their unorthodox character.

Another aspect of the originality and diversity of Islam in Turkey is the presence of numerous Sufi brotherhoods, mainly of Central Asian or Anatolian origin, which tend towards heterodoxy. These too have emerged from popular Islam, and constitute a centuries-old tradition. The word *tarikat* (path or way), of Arabic origin, designates – here as throughout the Muslim world – one of various brotherhoods, or orders, characterized by communal mystical practices. Officially banned since 1925, they were nevertheless the most successful in mobilising the Muslim masses at the beginning of the republican era, and survived as clandestine groups. They represent a means of socialization, religious grouping and moral integration, and act as mediators of political action. They are often organized, at least locally, around Sheikhs, who play an important role particularly in the southeastern part of the country.

The influence of the *Nakşibendiye* (or Naqshabandiyya) – probably the most widely diffused Muslim mystical order in the world – can thus be felt in Turkey, whereas it is not well represented in the Arab world. Founded in the sixteenth century in Transoxiania, it is characterized by a close attachment to Qur'anic law and to non-ostentatious forms of devotion, and the rejection of music and dance, which are replaced by *zikr*, an invocation of the divine in the form of a litany. This order upholds conservative theological positions and is marked also by its involvement in professional and political life. In Turkey its branches exert a moral and political influence on the electorate and the cadres of Islamist and nationalist parties, as well as on certain right-wing secular groupings.

The other brotherhoods – the *Qadiriya*, which developed largely in the southeast, the *Helvetiyye*, the *Rifâye*, the *Mevleviye* and the *Bektachiye* – are today in decline. New Islamic communities, or *cemaat*, have now taken over their role. Created in the second half of the twentieth century, they benefited from the reappearance of religious associations that had initially been outlawed. These 'neo-brotherhoods' rarely engage openly in mystical practices. Divided into a large number of branches, the *cemaat* today dominate the religious scene in Turkey. They are highly active in the domain of education, and are also the prime movers in building mosques and supporting imams. There are therefore mosques and madrassahs that do not depend on the *Diyanet* but are financed by the *cemaat* or simply by the faithful when the state does not get involved – as is the case in some remote villages or outlying suburbs.

The *Süleymanci*, who originate in the Balkans and claim to belong to the *Naksibendiye* brotherhood, represent the principal *cemaat* in Turkey. Unlike traditional Islamists, they have embraced technology and modernity. Their public action is principally centred on education and teaching, for their objective is to train an Islamist elite in order to place them later in high positions. To this end they select deserving but poor high school students and give them scholarships. There are more boarders in their residential schools than there are in public boarding schools. Often organized along the lines of a military order, these 'troops' are pushed into pursuing excellence.

Finally, there are the *Nurcus*, followers of the teachings of Bediüzzaman Said-i Nursi (1873–1960), who was born in eastern Turkey and was influenced by the *Nakşibendiye* brotherhood. Based on a spiritualism of Qur'anic inspiration, his teaching is above all a rejection of materialism, whether of the communist or capitalist variety. The *Nurcus* differ from fundamentalist movements inasmuch as they do not make *sharia* their rallying cry. The movement is dominated by a certain degree of positivism that tries to reconcile Islam and science, which they consider to be capable of contributing to universal harmony. The *Fethullahçi*, disciples of Fetullah Gülen (born 1938), constitute one of the principal branches to have emerged from the *Nurcus*. Like them, they seek to reconcile Islam and modernity, and to Islamise daily life by granting an important role to education and creating numerous centres in Turkey and among Turkish speakers throughout the world. This Islamic organization with a strongly nationalist flavour is among the most important in Turkey, where all of these movements exhibit a considerable degree of vigour.

A DYNAMIC SECTOR

The Islamic message and the traditional Muslim forces of social cohesion are in the process of being reappropriated to new purposes. Far from being archaic movements, the *tarikat* and the *cemaat* are noted for their worldly activities. They thus evince an important capacity for mobilising their adherents and clients at the ballot-box, either by striving to get one of their leaders elected or by lending political and financial support to certain candidates – and not always those of Islamist parties. In the southeast especially, the Sheikhs represent a significant proportion of the elected deputies. These movements of solidarity also act as interest groups and agents of social elevation, all the more so because their activists, products of their educational networks, have become increasingly middle class. The *cemaat* have, through a diversified network of associations, been able to exercise influence in industry, commerce, and communications.

Islam in Turkey has in recent years witnessed renewed vigour in all domains of society. Today it constitutes a varied and flourishing sector. Although the media have tended to take on a key role, traditional Islam makes room for more personal forms of faith and practice. An important dimension of the religious element in society lies in its effort to integrate concepts of modernity and technology, especially at the economic level, with the development of an Islamic economy and banking sector. Muslim players are entering spaces such as the cinema, hitherto reserved to the modernist elite. Similarly, the religious movements have shown themselves to be open to lively and varied intellectual debates, as witnessed by the multiplication of newspapers, publications, religious radio and television stations with diverse orientations and sensibilities. Generally, Islam is taking a full part in contemporary social debates in Turkey. Yet although the relationships between these groups and the authorities may fluctuate, on the whole they remain poor: the religious movements are regularly subject to repression and legal challenges for spreading 'reactionary propaganda'.

THE POLITICISATION OF ISLAM: ISLAMIST PARTIES AND RADICAL GROUPS

In spite of the secularity of the state, Islam today plays an integral part in the political life of the nation. With the transition to multiparty government in 1950, religion became a significant electoral issue, a form of concession to social demands used by all parties, especially by the conservative right. As for the Islamist parties, it was specifically Islam as a symbol of protest which they took as the basis for their political project. In 1970, Necmettin Erbakan founded the Milli Nizâm Partisi (MNP, National Order Party). After being banned in 1972, the party was replaced by the Milli Selamet Partisi (MSP, National Salvation Party) and then in 1983 by the Refah Partisi (RP, Welfare Party). This tradition, known under the name of Milli Görüş, or 'national vision', gravitates around the Muslim World League, under the religious and financial aegis of Saudi Arabia.

For contemporary Turkish political Islam, it is not a question of challenging the sociopolitical order or of bringing down a sacrilegious state, but rather of taking it over. Despite the execration of which it is regularly made the subject, there is no suggestion – apart from a few very isolated cases – that its activists will turn to radicalism. The few illegal and violent movements have a limited, even marginal, power base. In the southeast, the Hizbullah, which uses propaganda and armed struggle to demand an Islamic Kurdish state, has today been largely dismantled. The radical Islamic militants – mainly young people – have for the most part gone to fight on other fronts such as in Bosnia or Afghanistan. But although the attacks of November 2003 were isolated events, they do indicate that there are some active radical networks within Turkey itself.

On the other hand, the legal Islamist parties have gained crucial electoral importance, especially since the 1990s. How are we to explain the attraction that religious views hold for public opinion? In the 1970s the Islamic movement was supported largely by the conservative social classes of Anatolia. It continues to rely on the 'Anatolian lions', the upwardly mobile entrepreneurs of central Anatolia. The hypothesis that religious norms are being upheld by a group of people who were originally rural and marginalized but are now confronted by an urban milieu, remains plausible. This argument may also be extended to the segment of the population who is of Kurdish origin. But the Islamist movement also depends on new upwardly mobile social groups who are trying to escape their marginality by entering the modern social space. The basis of this movement thus extends to the urban, well-educated, and technocratic middle classes who are capable of rivalling the establishment both at the ideological and political level and in the business world. The diversity of the movement's base is not without a certain number of contradictions.

THE EXPERIENCE OF POWER: TRAP OR SPRINGBOARD?

Turkey is the first country in the region where an Islamist political grouping has come to power via the parliamentary route, without recourse to violence. The group won several victories at the ballot-box, first in the municipal elections of 1994, taking control of the principal cities of the land, and then in the parliamentary elections, winning 21.4 per cent of the votes in 1995 and 34.4 per cent in 2002. It was in 1996 that an Islamist party – the RP – for the first time headed up a coalition government, with the Right Way Party (DYP, on the centre right), although the movement had already had some limited experience of the corridors of power, since the MSP had participated in several coalitions during the 1970s.

The Islamists' access to power has elicited many hopes and fears as well as frictions, and even a power struggle with the military. The RP tried to pursue an 'Islamist foreign policy' that sought to move beyond the westernising orientation of Turkish foreign policy and forge ties of solidarity with Muslim countries, Central Asia and Turks living abroad, in order to create an Islamic common market. But the Muslim brotherhood proved to be an impossible dream, and this policy ended in disarray and humiliation. Caught in a web of institutional constraints, the RP was unable to break off ties with the 'Christian club' of Europe or with Israel.

At the local level, the RP announced that Hagia Sophia would be reconverted into a mosque, the sale of alcohol would be forbidden in certain neighbourhoods, men and women would be segregated on public transport, and a mosque would be built on Istanbul's Taksim square (a symbol of the secular republic). These reforms have not yet taken place, however, and the attempts to Islamize the public space have failed. Under pressure to give some token signs to their electoral base, the Islamists in power have had to make do with a number of symbolic statements: Islamizing the coats-of-arms of the cities of Istanbul and Ankara, restoring to pride of place an Ottoman past that had previously been kept hidden, or fighting – unsuccessfully for the moment – to have the wearing of headscarves permitted at university.

On some key points, however – such as the Kurdish question – the Islamists are indistinguishable from their predecessors. Their ambitious promises have given way to compromises. Their administrative approach has not differed substantially from those of other parties. The injection of a moral tone into political life, which was at the top of the list of their electoral promises, has been undertaken in a pragmatic manner. Just like the other parties, the RP has continued to govern in liberal fashion, based on a clientele system of distribution of state revenues.

Despite these concessions, and in particular the abandonment of several highly symbolic projects, on 28 February 1997 the military hierarchy issued an 'ultimatum'. It 'advised' the government to take measures against the 'rise of *sharia*' and to close down illegal Qur'anic courses and schools for imams and preachers – in short, to eradicate all Islamist activity and re-establish strict state control over all religious activities. The generals reminded the politicians that the army was empowered readily to resort to force to eliminate what the generals castigated under the generic label of *irtica*, or 'reaction'. Like it or not, Necmettin Erbakan, the RP Prime Minister, was obliged to implement these decisions and adopt policies he had vehemently denounced. At the institutional level, pressure upon the coalition soon grew so intense that the government had to resign in June 1997, after just a year in power. These measures were undoubtedly directed against the RP itself – a judicial investigation of the party led to its dissolution in January 1998.

Despite considerable hesitation and ambiguity, the ruling RP had been unable to change state structures or to fulfil the demands of the social groups it represented. It had been unable to institute *sharia*, or to meet the democratic and economic aspirations of its own support base. However, this experience served as an initiation for the Islamist movements in Turkey, and indeed in the whole world. After the fall of the RP from power, groups with an Islamist orientation did not withdraw from the public sphere or from political competition, as some had expected – quite the contrary. The successor to the RP, the FP (Fazilet Partisi, Virtue Party), banned in 2001, was in turn to be succeeded by a traditionalist party faithful to political Islam, the Saadet Partisi (Felicity Party), which met with spectacular failure in the elections of November 2002.

By contrast, the other party of Islamist inspiration, the reformist AKP (Adalet ve Kalkinma Partisi, Justice and Development Party) refused and refuses to define itself as Islamist. Preferring the label of conservative and liberal, it is close to the centre right, such that it would not be inappropriate to compare it to the Christian Democrats in Europe. Its success in the parliamentary elections of 2002 shows that this party conformed more closely to the expectations of the electorate, which seem rather to have disagreed with the alarmist assessment of 'reactionary danger' expressed by the military in 1997. Its strategy reflects the desire for integration: the AKP seems able to adapt itself to the rules of the game as far as competition and institutional order are concerned. This implies that its mission statement and its programme have been purged of anti-western, anti-Semitic and anti-establishmentarian elements, despite persistent traces of an ideology of systemic opposition.

While the AKP enjoys the necessary majority to carry out constitutional reforms, the steps that are under consideration – oriented towards 'less government' – have provoked some tensions with state institutions. These are not as severe, however, as they were under the Erbakan government. Intransigence has yielded to flexibility with respect to the EU, and even to a pro-European stance that puts them in a paradoxical situation. A party stigmatized by the Kemalist elites and regarded at times as a danger to secularity and democracy seems to be committed to realizing the age-old dream of Turkey's integration with Europe.

The experience of Islamists in power has shown the true pluralism of the Turkish political system, as well as its capacity to integrate opposition groups in spite of its ambiguities and limits. The successive dissolutions of Islamist parties by coup d'état (in 1971 and 1980) or by the Constitutional Court (in 1998 and 2001), in each case on the grounds of 'activities contrary to the principle of secularity and challenge to republican principles', reveal a generally antagonistic approach to religious questions. Following a rigid and obsolete conception of Kemalism, they reduce Islam to an anachronistic obscurantism and a betrayal of the nation, and make out that 'secularity' must be maintained by force of arms. As a result of recent developments, the social and political expressions of Islam appear to enjoy greater acceptance today, even if some still want to exclude them from the political scene. Will this sociological and cultural dimension ever succeed in emerging from the margins to which it has been relegated, and be accepted as a viable option? Will the political system be able to harness this major electoral force, and in particular to reap the benefits of the accompanying reformist dynamism?

TURKEY AND THE EUROPEAN UNION: FROM MIGRATION TO INTEGRATION?

Of the approximately 4 million Turkish expatriates worldwide, 3.3 million live in the member states of the European Union. Within its borders they make up the largest group of foreign nationals from outside the Community. The high visibility of what has been termed 'ethnic business', of the religious lives and political activities (posters and slogans in Turkish and in Kurdish) of Turks living in capital cities such as Berlin, Paris, Brussels and Amsterdam, and all the commonplaces about their 'ghettoisation' and 'non-integration' as compared to other foreign populations (such as those of north African origin), have contributed to the notion that if they have succeeded in blending economically into urban residential neighbourhoods, first-generation Turkish immigrants and their descendants have continued to embody an irreducible ethnic, religious, cultural, and political otherness that justifies keeping their country of origin out of the European Union.

In order to consider the way in which Turkish migration to Europe affects the debate on Turkey's joining the EU, we must pause to examine the most controversial points in the discussion. Over and above an economic analysis of the consequences of free circulation of European citizens of Turkish origin (not all citizens of the countries where they reside) if Turkey were to join the Union, there may be other factors more directly linked to the Turkish presence in Europe that can explain the dissonances that remain in a dialogue which, after all, has been going on for about 40 years.

The problems surrounding Turkey's accession to the EU are defined on the one hand by technical and bureaucratic reflections on economic, institutional, and legal reforms, and on the other by debates of a more political and passionate nature, of which the Copenhagen Criteria (human rights and democracy) represent the core. This debate, however, conceals certain cultural and symbolic elements that – even if invoked mainly in passing – nevertheless determine the basic script for the Turkish candidacy.

The principal obstacle has recently been put back on the agenda by the proposals of Valéry Giscard d'Estaing, president of the Convention on the Future of Europe. Speaking a few days after the elections of November 2002, which saw the triumph of a party that emerged from the Islamist movement (the AKP), he stressed the danger to the EU of admitting into its ranks a country that, in his view, does not belong in Europe. Such an opinion, rooted in a long history, presupposes an incompatibility between Turkey and Europe on account of their divergent values and histories, or antagonistic 'civilizations', to use a term no longer in context. Since its rise to power, and despite the most alarmist predictions, the government of Recep Tayyip Erdogan has steadily carried forward the 'pro-European' reforms promulgated in the summer of 2002.

This chapter examines the correlation between the presence in western Europe of a Turkish population that went there to work in the second half of the twentieth century, and the debate on Turkey's accession to Europe. A few historical details associated with the socio-economic profile of these migrants will enable us to articulate the unspoken elements of this discussion, and to pinpoint the main features of a debate that has begun to integrate the great issues of Turkish domestic politics into the discourse on enlargement of the Union.

TURKS AND PEOPLE OF TURKISH ORIGIN IN THE EUROPEAN UNION

Turkish immigration has been a reality in Europe since the 1960s. At the end of 2003 Turkish émigrés numbered more than 3 million (according to data provided by the Turkish

Ministry of Foreign Affairs in 2003). The largest concentration was in Germany (2,375,000, or 28 to 30 per cent of all foreigners), France (326,000, about 5 per cent of all foreigners), the Netherlands (323,000, or 15.5 per cent of foreigners), Belgium (134,000, about 7.7 per cent of foreigners), and Austria (133,000). Waves of migration also flowed to Switzerland (81,000), the United Kingdom (71,000), Denmark (49,000), Sweden (32,000) and Norway (11,000). Turkish emigrants additionally settled in the United States (102,000), Australia (89,000), Central Asia and the Middle East – primarily Saudi Arabia (108,000).

The first waves of migrant workers were part of an economic migration within the framework of international recruitment agreements, but in the early 1970s the majority emigrated for the purposes of family reunification. In the 1990s, the latter – mainly by way of marriage – continued to be one of the principal reasons for settling in Europe, along with requests for asylum. Thus between 1985 and 1995, 350,000 requests for asylum by Turkish citizens were recorded at the borders of the European Union. Demographic growth in Turkey was not unaffected by these relatively powerful waves of migration from Turkey to the EU. In fact, Turkish migration to Europe often followed an initial exodus within Turkey from the countryside to the cities – an exodus that became widespread in the second half of the 1970s. Since the 1980s, Istanbul has been the main destination for this movement, which has ensured the demographic development of that city.

In 1990, 59 per cent of Turks lived in cities and 41 per cent in the countryside (Deli, 2000). This is because a majority of those in the first wave of emigrants from Turkey were rural dwellers. Another important feature of Turkish migration has been the tendency to form migration networks. This means that migrants have followed others from their family or geographic region, which explains in part their concentration in particular urban settings.

In Germany, for instance, Turkish migrants are principally concentrated around the Ruhr basin, in North Rhine-Westphalia (where 35 per cent of all Turks in Germany live, and a quarter of all those residing in Europe) and in Berlin. In France they live in the Paris region, in Alsace, and in the Rhone-Alps region. The Turkish Kurds (statistically invisible because counted as Turks) have followed the same pattern of Turkish migration, although in their case there were political motivations as well (primarily as a result of the repression and guerrilla war that followed the coup d'état of 1980). They allegedly represent 25 per cent of the Turkish population living in Europe. In their case too, the migration patterns follow paths blazed by family and political networks from their places of origin, giving rise to a concentration in certain countries of the EU (Sweden, France and Germany). In the 1980s, Kurds from Iraq and Iran began to join those from Turkey.

The institutional history of the rapprochement between Europe and Turkey, built up progressively since 1963, is explicitly related to the phenomenon of migration. The association agreement signed in 1963, aiming in the long term at Turkey's accession to the EEC, expressed above all the desire of the Turkish government to reinforce its ties with Europe in order to sustain an economic development that had run into difficulties thanks to a fast-growing population of which 75 per cent of the active segment were, in 1962, employed in agriculture (Basri Elmas, 1998). Until the beginning of the 1970s, the Turkish labour force living in Europe thus contributed to financing the country's balance of payments deficit. Several studies have shown the impact of transfers of foreign currencies and savings from emigrant workers upon the economy of their country of origin, and particularly the effects of closing Europe's borders at the moment when demographic growth in Turkey reached a rate of a million births per year, and when domestic job creation was no longer sufficient (de Tapia, 1996).

Among the member states of the European Union, Germany was the principal destination from 1961 onwards – the year when a recruitment agreement was signed between the Federal Republic (West Germany) and Turkey. Initially,

60 per cent of emigration was by men between the ages of 20 and 40, but in certain cities (like Berlin) the electro-technical industry needed female workers. Arrivals and departures between 1964 and 1989 give some idea of the circulation between the two territories. During these years, 3,143,000 Turks entered Germany, and 1,899,000 left (Nauck, 1994). After 1973, family reunification (not included initially in the recruitment agreement) gradually replaced employment as the principal reason for immigration, and gave new impetus to the rise in Turkish population on German soil. The functionalist public perception of the presence of *Gastarbeiter* – guest workers – gave way little by little to a broader conception of their needs, expanded now to include those of their families.

By 1982, 1,580,000 Turks lived in Germany (in 1972 there had been 712,300). After a slight decline in numbers between 1980 and 1985 there was a new increase, the total reaching 2,053,546 by 31 December 1999 (making up 28 per cent of all foreigners). The numbers of Turkish migrants stabilized in the mid-1980s. The proportion of active workers among this population declined from 76.2 per cent in 1967 to 38.5 per cent in 1987, as did the fertility rate of Turkish women (from 4.3 children per woman in 1975 to 2.4 in 1985, only to rise again in the 1990s to 3.4 children per woman). Germany adopted various policies to encourage this tendency, but without any real effect. Assistance to those who wished to return to their homeland – a key component of German immigration policy between 1979 and 1985 – had only very limited success. The law of November 1983 on aid to returning immigrants (*Rückkehrhilfsgesetz*) in fact prolonged the rotation system set up in the early days of immigration. Yet an investigation carried out by the Centre for Turkish Studies in Essen shows that in 1988 83 per cent of Turkish citizens living in Germany did not intend to return to their country of origin. The law of 2 December 1981 limiting family reunification was another attempt – this one more effective – by the German government to influence migratory circulation between Turkey and Germany.

The political effort to limit the flow of migration to Europe has indirectly made its way into the debate about Turkey's entry into the EU. The potential free circulation within the Union of 68 million Turkish citizens, at a time when unemployment in Turkey itself remains high, has fed the opposition to European enlargement. Given the ageing population and the decline in birth rate that characterizes a majority of member states, the fear of a return of mass migration (the estimates for 2004 placed Turkey's population at 90 million), this time of fully-fledged citizens of Europe, is linked to the controversial effort to adopt a common immigration policy for the EU. From the signing of the Schengen agreement by the Benelux countries, France and Germany in 1985 to the coming into force of the Treaty of Amsterdam on 1 May 1999, the countries concerned have undertaken to harmonize their laws and national policies on immigration matters. The effort to address this question on a Community-wide scale has had only relative success and is limited to the intergovernmental level, for the national delegations sought to limit the competence of the Community when they were drafting the treaty.

The free circulation of workers is, however, entrenched in the Treaty of Rome (articles 48, 49, and 50) and has been included in the association agreement with Turkey known as the Treaty of Ankara (1963). It has never been fully implemented, however, despite its reaffirmation in 1974 by an additional protocol. Initially the intention was to introduce the policy in a progressive, graduated fashion (between December 1976 and November 1986), but the free circulation of Turkish workers was radically rejected as a medium-term prospect with the closure of European borders to immigration in 1973-74. Nor does it reappear in the customs union agreement.

The potential emigration of a poorly-qualified Turkish workforce is obviously a fundamental consideration in this issue – all the more so since factors that obtained in the 1960s are still present. The disparities between urban and rural areas have further increased, the population is growing at a rate of

2 per cent annually, the high unemployment rate now affects those who are in a weak or precarious situation, especially women and young people, and the average salary is constantly declining. For many Turks the option of emigrating continues to have great appeal.

DIVERSIFICATION OF PROFILES AND PROCESSES

Since the early 1960s, important changes have taken place in the consumer and savings patterns among people of Turkish origin living in Europe. These changes permit us to measure the transition of the perception of their presence in Europe from as a temporary sojourn to as a lifetime project definitively rooted in their new place of residence. The net annual revenue of active workers has risen, and since the second half of the 1980s their incomes have no longer been transferred home to Turkey but spent (or invested) in the country of residence. Logically, then, consumer spending and investments locally rose as the prospects of returning declined. In a reunified Germany, the Turkish entrepreneurial class turned to the new states (*Länder*), and the range of activities traditionally defined as 'ethnic' diversified considerably. In 1992, the contribution of Turks to a 'solidarity surcharge' (*Solidaritätsangabe*) instituted by the government for the 'reconstruction' of the eastern states amounted to 470 million Deutschemarks.

This differentiation of profiles and projects calls for a carefully balanced analysis. In fact, just as the profile of European societies varies, so the make-up of the immigrant population can hardly be regarded as a homogeneous aggregate, defined exclusively by a supposed tendency to remain enclosed within their own communities. In Germany, the labels favoured by politicians, the press and the administration for designating these segments of the population speak volumes about the difficulties of grasping the multiple positions and complex sources of identity that define them. The children and grandchildren of 'guest workers' were labelled 'foreign residents' and, more recently, 'German Turks'. In Germany, as in the rest of the Union, although they continue to be treated as foreigners, they nevertheless participate in many diverse sectors of social life and, more and more often, choose to take up the nationality of their place of residence. As economic players, bearers of civic rights in some cases and of social rights in most, investors, academics, intellectuals, politicians and artists, they are to be found alongside nationals even though they do not always enjoy the same legal status.

The legal issue is also in the process of evolution. Since 1 January 2000, a relaxation of Germany's legislation concerning access to citizenship – one of the most problematical in Europe in terms of requirements and the length of the process – has allowed children born in the Federal Republic to parents of foreign origin to claim German nationality from their birth, and to choose at the age of 23 between this one and the nationality of the parents. Nevertheless, in almost all the member states, the highly diversified population that makes up the group identified as 'Turkish' continues to be perceived by the public authorities and by the European imagination as following an essentially 'communitarian' dynamic – one characterized by a population turned inward upon itself, satisfied with this isolation and reluctant or hostile with regard to the prospects of participating in the so-called 'host' societies.

If it is important to tie the developments in Turkish migratory patterns to the opportunities offered by the great centres of European employment, their relationship to the internal politics of their home country should not be underestimated. The coups of 1960, 1971 and 1980, and the conflict in eastern Turkey, have all been additional factors in the decision to emigrate, taken by people as much for economic as for political reasons, even if all migrants initially left without any intention of resettling permanently. In many respects, the creation of a web of associations that structure the lives of Turks in Europe reflects this ongoing interaction with the country of origin, and the transnational dynamic that animates the various kinds of Turkish networks (entrepreneurs, associations, political militants, intellectuals, students, etc.).

Other aspects for analysis (the organization and diffusion of media in Turkish, the militancy of the left, religious groupings) help shed light on this transnational perspective, in which the importance of the first generation's country of origin continues to play a central role even for the third generation, who were not born in Turkey but only spend their holidays there.

There is often talk of an ambiguous process of integration as far as Turks are concerned, indicating a tension between participation in the new country's economic and political processes on the one hand, and the maintenance of a strong sense of cohesion among themselves on the other. This has been attributed to their lower level of education and weaker social mobility, as compared to other groups of immigrants, in particular with reference to indicators such as intermarriage and language-learning. The range of areas in which they become involved, and the many different forms their activities take, are not limited to lobbying on foreign policy issues but reveal a symbolically rich array of activities attesting to individual and collective commitments in many different national territories. These activities may find support from family connections, religious convictions or political militancy.

The Turkish network of associations, established in Germany since the 1970s, reflects for example the entire range of political tendencies present in Turkey. This network continues to this day to maintain the distinctions among currents of thought that follow closely those in the home country – which becomes evident at pre-election meetings, for example. Continuing the conflict and violence between Turks and Kurds, or the rivalries between the Kemalists and Islamists, among émigré communities is part of this transnational link between Turkey and the host states in Europe.

The Turkish state, for its part, is not indifferent to these 'transnational communities' made up of Turks and Kurds in the European diaspora. Moreover, the freedom of expression and political organization found in Europe has contributed to raising political awareness, in certain quarters, of ethnic or religious loyalties. Expressions of political commitment do not stop at national borders. Exile, too, can become a resource for the two public enemies of the army and the Turkish state – Kurdish nationalism and Islamism – and can render it possible to organize a transnational mobilization (Amiraux, 2001).

KURDS LIVING IN EXILE IN EUROPE

The Kurds living in Europe are perhaps the best example of this dynamic within the diaspora. There are two crucial elements at the heart of Kurdish nationalist demands: language and territory. The close links between exile and Kurdish nationalism, present since the early twentieth century, have mutually reinforced each other since the mid-1980s, supported by access to new tools of communication (media, audiovisual aids, the Internet) that escape the censorship of the Turkish state, as well as to a much more free realm of expression that opens the door to publications in Kurdish (in particular from Sweden).

Closer ties between different areas of settlement have permitted a Kurdish political consciousness to emerge. The collection of funds, the recruitment of militants or even combatants, the creation of a form of non-territorial mobilization – Europe as a whole has and European states individually have opened up real opportunities for redeployment to Kurdish opposition movements (van Bruinessen, 2000).

This has led in particular to a change in the scale on which they express their demands. Members of the public who have been moved by the Kurdish cause are more and more widespread and diverse (western European political leaders, intellectuals, academics, NGOs), and the strength of the political message has therefore intensified. The Kurdish institutes of Paris (founded in 1983), Berlin (1994) and Brussels (1989), and the Parliament in exile (founded in 1983), which are more recent institutions, have also functioned as sources of publicity. The media, and in particular

Med-TV, a satellite television station broadcasting from Great Britain between 1995 and its banning in 1999, helped create platforms for discussion and communication about the Kurdish situation in Turkey, and favoured the inclusion of new militants, for the most part non-Kurds. The militants were able, from their base in Europe, to develop a most effective lobby both at national government level and at the European institutions. Thus, for instance, human rights activists systematically brought legal action against the Turkish state at the European Court of Human Rights (Bertrand and Rigoni, 2000).

Today, in the debate about Turkey's accession to the Union, the Kurdish question – which has become a European question – remains the most salient argument, for which the diaspora has constituted a sounding-board. Its weighty effect on European politics has been felt on several occasions, as may be seen in the banning of the PKK (Kurdistan Workers' Party) in Germany and the interruption of arms sales to the Turkish government by the German authorities. Recent concessions by the Turkish government, notably with regard to the Kurdish language, show the power of European influence upon Turkish internal policy decisions. Clearly in this case the migrant communities in Europe were mobilized on behalf of specific policy demands for their country of origin rather than in their host countries.

TURKISH EMIGRATION: AN OBSTACLE TO INTEGRATION?

In respect of the phenomenon of Turkish migration, is it possible to declare whether it advances or hinders Turkey's membership in the European Union? The debate on enlargement of the Union to include Turkey, while regularly feeding polemics, is not a central one within Europe's borders (but is it even so in Turkey?). But the discussion cannot easily ignore all those citizens of Turkey who, in Europe perhaps more than in Turkey, have learned the lessons of democracy and pluralism. It would be important therefore to consider more systematically the effects on Turkey of certain decisions taken by European states concerning minorities such as the

Alevis. Nor ought we to ignore the effects on Turkish residents in Europe if Turkey were to be shut out, or the wider consequences of a 'culturalist' conception of European citizenship.

We have seen that there is a complex and intricate link between the proposed admission of Turkey and the reticence of the principal actors in this rapprochement to make a permanent commitment to the project of enlargement. The familiarity that has resulted from the experience of migration, and the intensity of *multiple* transnational ties, seem to be absent from the current discussions. These tend instead to stress the distance between Europe and an 'other' that, although a near neighbour with which it has been interacting on a daily basis ever since the recruitment agreements came into effect, Europe refuses to integrate politically in the medium term.

In this rejection of Turkey there is a considerable element of irrational fear inspired and to some extent sustained directly by that very experience of cohabitation. The possibility of restricting Europe to a 'Christian club' and rejecting the legitimacy of Turkey's candidacy has defined the terms of the fundamental debate, always announced but never achieved, concerning the cultural bases of the European project, now that a signed, definitive accord has been concluded concerning political principles such as the rule of law and democratic institutions. Implicit agenda for candidacy to the EU should become explicit requirements. In this quest for identity to which Europe hesitates to commit itself, perhaps the Turks residing within her borders have a role to play, or at the very least a voice to contribute.

THE KURDISH QUESTION: CAN IT BE SOLVED WITHIN EUROPE?

Since the foundation of the Turkish Republic in 1923, the Kurdish question has been a chronic source of instability and violence in the country. From 1924 to 1938, Kurdistan saw several revolts that seriously weakened the state's power. In the 1970s, certain Kurdish groups, such as the PKK (Kurdistan Workers' Party), turned to violent struggle. The guerrilla war launched by this organization in 1984 continued until 2000. During this period, the Kurdish question – along with that of Cyprus – was the principal factor that influenced Turkish foreign policy. The support given by Damascus to the PKK provoked overt tensions between Syria and Turkey. Similarly, the creation after the Gulf War (1991) of a 'protective zone' in Iraqi Kurdistan, which was used as a rear base by the PKK, served as a pretext for repeated Turkish military incursions. Ankara made it perfectly clear that the creation of a viable Kurdish entity within Iraq, and the return of Kurds who had been sent into exile by Saddam Hussein's regime to the city of Kirkuk, which Ankara considered to be a Turkmen – and therefore a Turkish – city, would constitute a *casus belli*.

A resolution of this question was not made one of the explicit preconditions for Turkey's accession to the European Union. Like the Cyprus question, however, its significance lies rather in what is implicit, what is left unsaid and unwritten. It is clear that the absence of a solution to this matter means that there is an ever-present risk of a new civil war, the shockwaves of which would be felt in Europe, as was the case during the decade of the 1990s. The danger that the PKK – first

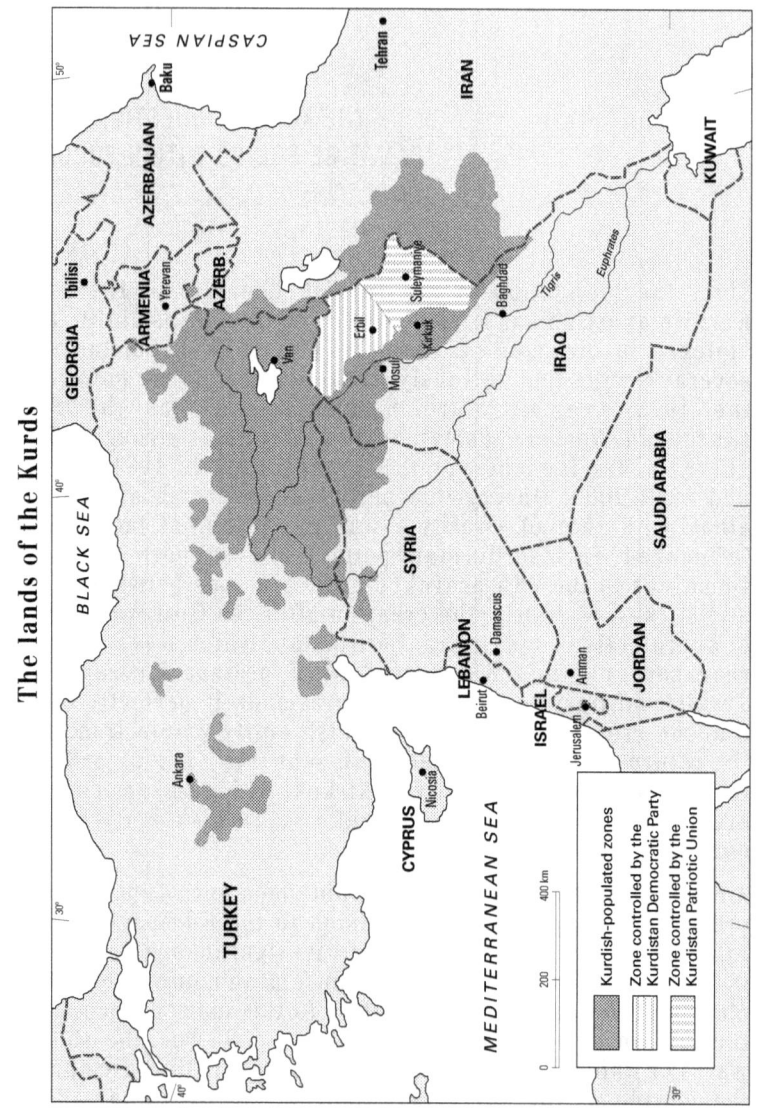

The lands of the Kurds

rebaptised KADEK (Congress for Freedom and Democracy in Kurdistan), and then Kongra Gel (People's Congress) – might again turn to armed struggle if negotiations for satisfying Kurdish demands within the framework of Turkish territorial integrity are not opened, must therefore be taken very seriously indeed. Similarly, if negotiations were not opened, the multinational dimension of the Kurdish question would oblige an enlarged Europe to become more involved in the Middle East.

Only half of the 25 million Kurds live in Turkey. The Turkish Kurds for the most part maintain emotionally strong relations with the Kurds of Iran (8 million), Iraq (more than 4 million) and Syria (1 million). We must not lose sight of the fact that the hostility that since the end of the Gulf War has dogged relations between Washington and Ankara has to do on the one hand with the presence of several thousand Turkish Kurd fighters in Iraqi Kurdistan, and on the other with the status of the Iraqi Kurds – two issues that naturally cannot be ignored by Europe.

In this chapter we first present a few historical pointers that help shed light on the development of this question since 1923. These facts are all the more important because they shape the attitudes and subjectivities that prevail both in Ankara and within the Kurdish movement. Secondly, we analyse the situation of 'neither peace nor war' which has existed since the arrest of Abdullah Öcalan, leader of the PKK/KADEK, in 1999. Finally, we emphasize the probable impact of this question on the negotiation process between Turkey and the European Union.

THE GENEALOGY OF A NATIONAL CONFLICT: FROM ALLIANCE TO RUPTURE

The Kurdish question springs from the emergence of Kurdish nationalism at the end of the Ottoman Empire. This movement first developed in opposition to or interaction with other nationalisms, such as Armenian and Turkish. Like the other nationalisms within the Ottoman Empire, it was an ideology that emerged primarily among the westernised elites, having initially little impact on the urban populations or, *a fortiori*, rural ones. For these latter groups, the lines of demarcation between 'us' and 'them' were mainly religious, separating and even opposing Muslims and Christians. This solidarity constituted one of the principal reasons for the alliance between Kurdish dignitaries and the power of the Committee of Union and Progress during World War I and at the time of the Armenian genocide, in which certain urban and tribal Kurdish militias played a significant part.

In 1920 the Treaty of Sèvres recognized the possibility of creating a Kurdish state. Despite the efforts of a nationalist elite, however, the majority of Kurdish leaders remained loyal to the Kemalist resistance against the occupying forces (Greeks, British, French and Italian). Their fear of seeing the birth of an Armenian state, the creation of which was decided by the same treaty, was the principal reason for this new alliance – but they were also seduced by the objective of 'protection and preservation of the caliphate' by which General Mustafa Kemal justified the War of Independence (1919–22). Similarly, the promises of Turkish-Kurdish brotherhood that Kemal made in a series of declarations and letters seemed to them to modify to their advantage the alliance with the state. Finally, Kemal committed himself to preserving the unity of Ottoman Kurdistan and to recovering the *vilaya* of Mosul (present-day Iraqi Kurdistan), then occupied by the British.

The end of the War of Independence, the signing of the Treaty of Lausanne, and the foundation of the Republic (1923), however, rapidly changed the state of affairs. The Kemalist forces were compelled to accept the annexation of Mosul to Iraq. So in addition to the division of the Kurds between the Ottoman and the Persian Empires since 1639, there was now a new fragmentation. The presence of Kurds in Syria, a former Ottoman territory, complicated matters further. The militarization of the frontiers aggravated the consequences of this new division. Henceforth, Kurds would be divided by national borders, and their profile identity would be fragmented: yet they would never cease defying the limits set by these definitions, and every armed protest mobilized people well beyond the frontiers of a single state. During the decades that followed World War I, Kurdish nationalism would manage this explosion by creating common references, symbols and myths – a historiography, a flag, a map and a national anthem – thus providing the nation with a symbolic unity.

This new division of Kurdistan was not, however, the only factor leading to radicalisation among Kurdish nationalists. The evolution of the Kemalist state played an equally important role. Very soon, Kemal abandoned his promises to preserve Islam and the caliphate, and instead energetically launched a westernising political programme. If he adopted Islam as one of the components of national identity, it was only by default. The process of 'Islamization' in Turkey, carried out by means of the extermination or expulsion of Christians, went hand in hand with a strong-armed policy of secularization that ended with the abolition of the caliphate in 1924 and the prohibition of the religious fraternities in 1925.

This development gave rise among Kurds to a sense that their contract with the Turks – hitherto justified by the brotherhood of all Muslim peoples – had come to an end. Moreover, the promises of Turkish-Kurdish brotherhood during the War of Independence gave way to an exclusivist Turkish nationalism. The young republic did not recognize any identity other than Turkish. Either it simply denied the existence of the Kurds, or it saw 'Kurdishness' as 'feudal' and 'reactionary' and the Kurds as an 'oppressive' ethnic group and class, the historical mission of which was, in its view, to exploit and destroy progressive and revolutionary 'Turkishness'.

As a result of this policy, a series of revolts broke out, of which three (those of 1925, 1927-30, and 1936-39) required the mobilization of more than 50,000 soldiers. Kurdistan was completely militarized and placed under the control of 'general inspectors', all Kurdish cultural expression was forbidden, and several laws were passed to dismantle 'zones inhabited by populations not belonging to the Turkish culture'.

THE YEARS OF SILENCE AND OF RENEWAL

The two subsequent decades saw the exhaustion of the Kurdish movement and a relative integration of some of its dignitaries, achieved thanks to a transition to political pluralism in 1946 and to the changes of 1950 that brought a liberal party to power. Some nationalists were able to take advantage of a certain room for manoeuvre, no matter how small, in return for their formal respect for the rituals of Kemalist unanimity. The Turkish political system managed this *de facto* compromise so well that it never came to the formulation of explicit, collective demands.

From the 1960s onward, however, two factors pushed the Kurdish nationalists to try to acquire greater visibility: the revolt of Mustafa Barzani in Iraqi Kurdistan (1961–75) and the birth of a robust student movement within Turkey itself, which offered Kurdish youths born after the Kemalist repression a new ideology of global protest. The ultimate rejection of the new generation's demands – such as recognition of the Kurdish fact and cultural rights, and economic development – by Turkish political authorities only pushed them more strongly towards overt opposition. This radicalisation continued after the military *pronunciamiento* of 12 March 1971 through a process of fragmentation that gave rise, among others, to the PKK, the initial objective of which was to constitute a Kurdish socialist state and to unify the Middle East.

The violence undertaken by this organization between 1977 and 1980 against the other Kurdish organizations earned it a bad reputation among the Kurdish people. But the attitude of the new military regime (1980–83), which declared that Kurdishness was a disease that required Kemalist treatment, revived its prestige. The PKK fled to Syria and then Lebanon, where it reconstituted its forces in order to take part in the civil war, and acquired some real military experience. On 15 August 1984 it returned to Turkey and launched a guerrilla war that was to last 15 years and cost the lives of about 40,000 victims (of whom about 5,000 were members of the security forces and as many again were civilians). In spite of its great brutality, the war was considered by the youth and by a large part of the urban Kurdish population a way of redressing the injustices committed towards Kurds – and the fighters' ranks grew from year to year.

The authorities' response to the guerrilla war, infinitely better organized than any of the earlier Kurdish protests, was to remilitarize the Kurdish region. From 1987 onward, a 'governorate' of a proconsular type was established, and a militia was created – essentially tribal in nature – composed today of nearly 100,000 men. Fulfilling the 'doctrine of low-intensity counter-insurrection' adopted at the beginning of the 1990s, thousands of villages and hamlets as well as a few cities were destroyed, giving rise to the displacement of several million people. The paramilitary forces, among which were the bands of the radical right as well as groups of Islamist militants, the Hizbullahi, tolerated and armed by the authorities, proceeded to carry out nearly 2,000 extrajudicial executions, including the executions of Kurdish nationalists who had no link with the PKK. By evoking the 'threat of separatist terrorism', the army and the National Security Council – a significant organ of power dominated by the army – were enabled to enjoy the support of almost the entire political class and civil and judicial establishment.

Finally, during this period legal Kurdish political parties saw the light of day. If their successive prohibitions and the repression of their members did not permit them to survive long-term, to obtain the 10 per cent of the votes needed to enter the National Assembly, or to elaborate a political programme distinct from that of the PKK, they nevertheless succeeded in gaining power in some Kurdish municipalities.

The arrest of the PKK chief Abdullah Öcalan in February 1999 at the Greek embassy in Kenya, where he had fled, opened up a new phase in the history of the party and of the Kurds in Turkey. Öcalan offered apologies for the violence perpetrated by his party over the previous 15 years and, in exchange for the recognition of Kurdish cultural rights, proposed a new agreement preserving the integrity of Turkey and called for an end to the armed struggle. In spite of some sporadic confrontations, his decision was on the whole supported by his organization.

A SITUATION THAT IS 'NEITHER PEACE NOR WAR'

With the cessation of hostilities, the Kurdish question seems no longer to be a source of political instability or massive violence. However, in the long run it will be difficult to maintain the present state of equilibrium, which might be said to be hanging by a thread. For the present situation is neither more nor less than a total standstill. Certainly, since 2000 the state of siege that prevailed in the Kurdish cities has been lifted and some reforms concerning 'minority languages' have been adopted in order to fulfil the Copenhagen Criteria, which candidate countries of the European Union have to meet before they can join. But human rights violations continue, and the reforms, which in any case fall short of Kurdish expectations, are being implemented only in an overly timorous manner where they are implemented at all.

Among the 'third package' of reforms launched in August 2002, for instance, Ankara authorized the teaching of 'local' languages in private institutions – but the national Ministry of Education was designated as the only body capable of granting diplomas in the subject. Several thousand students demanding courses in their Kurdish mother tongue were arrested and in some cases tortured and expelled from their institutes. Broadcasts in 'local languages' on radio and television were permitted, but they were subject to constraints that in fact rendered them impossible (the prohibition of broadcasting on private wavelengths, broadcasts on public stations were limited to a few hours a week and only very late in the evening, there was an obligation to provide subtitling or complete translation, etc.). Such requirements are, after all, quite unnecessary since households are able to tune in to Kurdish stations broadcasting via satellite and access hundreds of websites based in Europe. Prohibitions concerning Kurdish given names have been upheld and

Kurdish politicians holding meetings in the local language continue to be challenged by law enforcement agencies. Finally, Ankara does not conceal the fact that it considers all Kurdish legal and political representation as grave a menace to 'national security' as 'separatist terrorism'.

In addition to this standstill, there is not surprisingly a mood of considerable frustration that prevails in Kurdish regions and could potentially lead to violence. Although a large part of the urban population wants no such recourse to violence, that does not seem to be the case among the younger generations. Here, as elsewhere in the Middle East, the rural exodus accelerated by the years of war has helped to politicise new generations of ever-younger militants at a more rapid rate. The continued attacks against the combatants of the PKK, despite their having unanimously declared the end of the armed struggle, are pushing many 15- or 16-year-old youths to 'take up the torch' of the elders to 'avenge the martyrs'. The leaders of the PKK/KADEK cannot ignore this impatience without running the risk that rival organizations will emerge.

Finally, the uncertainties throughout the Middle East born of the Iraq War should be taken into consideration. The consequences of these have been both to normalize relations between Iraqi Kurds and the PKK/KADEK, two factions which in the past have many times flown at each other's throat, and to place the PKK/KADEK in a most precarious situation. Given the risks of a new rapprochement between Washington and Ankara, Öcalan's organization – which counts more than 5,000 combatants – might be tempted to turn its attention entirely to Turkish Kurdistan.

THE KURDISH QUESTION AND EUROPEAN CANDIDACY

So the Kurdish question, removed from the negotiations between Ankara and Brussels thanks to the end of armed struggle decreed by the PKK, might, in the short or medium term, return to the forefront by violent means. Turkey's accession to the EU may yet be impeded by a number of other more or less neglected issues: the Cyprus question, acknowledgment of the Armenian genocide, or support for Kemalism as the official and thus mandatory ideology of the Turkish republic and its citizens. More than 3 million people from Turkey living in Europe, who in the past had brought the Kurdish question right into the heart of Europe, would not remain indifferent to such a development.

This scenario is not, however, inevitable. Ankara's acknowledgment of the existence of its 12 million Kurdish citizens as a specific segment of its population; an audacious decentralization conferring wide powers on the provinces; the recognition of Kurdish political parties or Kurdish branches of 'national' political parties; the abandonment of Kemalism's status as official ideology; and finally the creation, on the South African model, of a 'Truth and Reconciliation' commission entrusted with bringing to light the massive violations of human rights committed in Kurdish regions – all this might considerably improve the image of Turkey in Europe and hasten its integration, while at the same time going a significant way towards meeting the expectations of the Kurds.

European integration might thus provide an institutional framework for and trust in the state and Kurdish institutions, at least among those who renounce armed struggle in return for their legalization. The models available in this regard are not lacking. A number of European countries recognize the cultural plurality of their societies, and decentralization permits them at various levels to delegate a number of prerogatives to regional entities or local authorities. Several countries, from Spain to Finland, also recognize the legality of 'particularist' parties. And after all, no European country has an official ideology to which the constitution obliges citizens to adhere and which alone defines citizenship, as is the case in Turkey.

Although these reforms are modest in themselves, nothing could be more radical in the context of present-day Turkey. They constitute the basis for a *de facto* consensus among Kurdish groups and the liberal Turkish pro-European camp.

Such a programme would most certainly strengthen Turkey's position in its negotiations with Brussels, and in return, by altering the rigid positions that set the terms of all debate in Turkey today, it would undoubtedly permit the development of new integrative mechanisms among the Kurds.

Finally, this new framework would permit the Kurds of Turkey to enter into a process of democratisation, to put an end to the cult of their leader, hardly to be distinguished from the cult the Turkish Republic pays to its founder. Leaving behind their tragic vision of history, Kurds would be able to give a non-conflictual meaning to their sense of dual identity as citizens of a Turkey within Europe, and members of a national, transborder community for which they could serve as a model. Conversely, the elaboration in due course of a common European policy would mean that Ankara would renounce all irredentist demands (namely concerning Iraqi Kurdistan, and more particularly the city of Kirkuk) and establish relations of trust with Kurds of other countries who would no longer regard them as the enemy, as is still the case today among Iraqi Kurds.

It is self-evident, however, that the implementation of such reforms requires on the one hand a radical change in the very structures of Turkish power (namely, the end of the military's political role), and on the other the abandonment of the image of Turkey as a fortress under siege, the survival of which depends on its constant mobilization against enemies both within and without. The arguments for defending the status quo in Cyprus or for intervention in Iraqi Kurdistan (the refusal to allow Turkish areas to be encircled, the 'doctrine of national security as guarantor of the future of the Turkish nation', etc.), and the vehemence that dominates the discussions about the adoption or non-adoption of the reforms demanded by Brussels, show that Ankara still has a long way to go towards the fulfilment of this objective.

contexts

THE OTTOMAN EMPIRE — 93
ROBERT MANTRAN

MUSTAFA KEMAL ATATÜRK — 119
ROBERT MANTRAN

THE GENESIS OF THE IDEA OF EUROPE — 131
JEAN-BAPTISTE DUROSELLE

THE IDEA OF EUROPE SINCE 1945 — 149
ALFRED GROSSER

THE ARMENIAN GENOCIDE — 163
CHRISTOPHE CHICLET

THE CYPRIOT QUESTION — 173
ALI KAZANCIGIL

MAKARIOS III — 181
ZAKHOS PAPAZAKHARIOU

Bibliography — 185
Further Internet Resources — 189
Glossary — 191
Index — 195

The Ottoman Empire

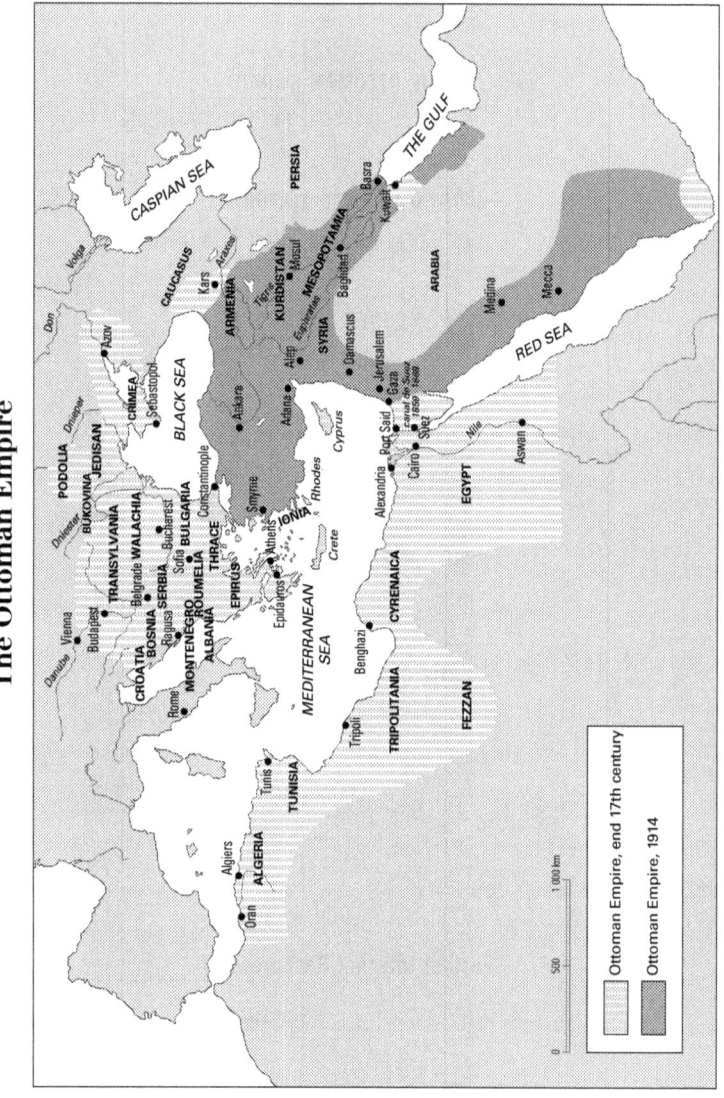

THE OTTOMAN EMPIRE
ROBERT MANTRAN

Built up gradually at the beginning of the fourteenth century on the ruins of the Seljuk state of Anatolia, and then in the fifteenth century on those of the Byzantine Empire, the Ottoman state became one of the major powers of Europe and the Near East after the conquest of Constantinople (29 May 1453). Well administered and endowed with a strong army, the empire posed a serious and constant threat to the European powers throughout the sixteenth century and part of the seventeenth. Master of the Mediterranean, North Africa, the Balkans, the Near East and the shores of the Black Sea, it was the last of the great empires of the Old World and may be considered the successor of the Roman, Byzantine, and Arab empires. Its political domination, more liberal and tolerant than is generally believed, was accompanied by an intellectual and artistic flowering that earned the reign of Süleyman the Magnificent its well-deserved reputation.

As a result of its lack of will or ability to adapt itself to the new economic conditions of Europe, and in particular to industry, and surrounded by neighbours – especially Russia – who were jealous of its power, the Ottoman Empire experienced reversals of fortune from the eighteenth century onward that led it to submit to western domination in economic and later in political matters. The 'Eastern question' in the nineteenth century consisted essentially in the efforts of some European states to dismember the Empire and divide up the spoils. This project succeeded almost completely. Thanks to Mustafa Kemal, however, the territory of Anatolia was preserved intact and a new Turkish state was created in 1923, bringing the Ottoman Empire definitively to an end.

THE ORIGINS OF THE OTTOMAN EMPIRE

The Seljuk Turkish sultanate of Asia Minor (or Anatolia) succeeded in establishing its dominion over most of the Anatolian peninsula in the course of the twelfth century, leaving the Byzantines only its westernmost part. After a period of splendour during the first third of the thirteenth century, the sultanate found itself facing several serious problems that would eventually lead to its downfall. By the middle of the thirteenth century, disputes over succession had shaken the unity and centralisation of the government, leading to a weakening of its power at the very moment when the Empire was facing the invasion of the Mongol Ilkhans, heirs in the Near East to the empire of Genghis Khan. Victorious, the Mongols made the entire eastern part of Anatolia into their protectorate. Elsewhere, internecine quarrels and intrigues among the viziers contributed to annihilating the Sultans' power. Into this declining state came the Turkmen tribes, whom the Seljuk Sultans had gradually settled a century earlier along the borders of the Byzantine-Turkish regions. These tribes or groups of tribes were more or less well assimilated in the Turco-Muslim world and had preserved a combative spirit that the Sultans strove to direct against the Byzantine Empire. Moreover, they were inspired by Muslim religious sentiment, albeit still impregnated with shamanism and under the leadership of the religious fraternities. Moved by proselytism, they willingly engaged in struggles against Christians.

Small Autonomous Emirates (Thirteenth Century)

Taking advantage of the weakening of the Seljuk rulers, these tribes constituted autonomous emirates (*beylik*) on the outskirts of the sultanate, particularly towards the west. They became fully independent at the end of the thirteenth century. The western emirates were determined to conquer Byzantine territories – those of the centre (for example, the emirate of Karaman) sought to acquire the Seljuk lands. But none of them was strong enough to prevail over the others. Nevertheless, the actions of the western emirates, although not coordinated, led to the disappearance of Byzantine authority in western Asia Minor, which, around 1340, came entirely under Turkish power.

It was one of these emirates, governed in the early fourteenth century by Osman (Outeman), which under the leadership of his successors was to have a remarkable future as the Ottoman Empire. For a long time, the origins of the Ottomans and their history –at least before the fourteenth century – remained obscure, since until recently historians had only incomplete sources available, or relied on later Turkish sources written to glorify the Ottoman dynasty. Newly available documents, mainly in Ottoman and European archives, and a critical analysis of chronicles have now made possible a better grasp of Ottoman history.

The tribe from whence the Ottoman dynasty issued belonged to the Oguz branch of the Turks. It had come from Central Asia either at the same time as the Seljuks or, more likely, a little later, having been pushed westwards by the Mongols in the beginning or middle of the thirteenth century. We know little about the first tribal leaders in Anatolia, who have been the subject of countless legends or later historical inventions. One of them, Ertughrul, seems to have been given the region of Seuyut (Söğüt) on the Sakarya River around 1260, and to have been entrusted with its defence against the Byzantines if not with mounting an offensive against them. At his death in around 1290, his son Osman took over the emirate and moved without delay to attack the Greeks. Perhaps Osman, like his son Orkhan after him, belonged to the Ghazi fraternity, a religious and military group whose main objective was to fight for the Muslim faith and for its triumph. It is in any event beyond doubt that the influence of religion was very strong on the first leaders of the dynasty.

The Conquests of Osman and His Son (1290-1362)

Even before the end of the thirteenth century, Osman had brought the eastern part of Byzantine Bithynia under his control. His conquests, although somewhat limited, earned him the support of other Turks or Turkmens who wished to fight for Islam as well as to share in the spoils. In around 1317 Osman (d. c.1326) yielded command of his little group to his son Orkhan, who continued the campaign to capture Byzantine cities – Brousse (1326), Nicaea (1330 or 1331) and Nicomedia (1337) – and to gain control of the neighbouring emirate of Karasi, located on the shores of the Sea of Marmara and the Dardanelles. This conquest gave Orkhan possession of a long coastline, well situated in relation to the European territories of Byzantium. He had already set up an embryonic form of administration in the conquered lands, had given his followers the principal posts, and had organized an army made up of regular units (in particular the cavalry) and irregular troops (infantrymen or *azab*, and cavalrymen or *akinji*).

The road to Europe had been opened up to the Ottomans by the Greeks themselves. In fact, after the death of the *Basileus* Andronicus III (1341), First Minister John Cantacuzenus, wishing to accede to the throne in place of the heir John V Palaeologus, appealed to Emir Umur of Aydin, whose troops had entered Thrace in 1343 and then in 1345. Upon the death of Umur, Cantacuzenus turned to Orkhan, to whom he had given his daughter Theodora in marriage (in around 1345–46). Orkhan sent soldiers to Thrace under the command of his son Süleyman. In March 1354 an earthquake destroyed the fortifications of Gallipoli and Süleyman captured the city, which Orkhan refused to surrender to John Cantacuzenus. The latter renounced his claim to the imperial throne soon thereafter, but Süleyman continued his march on eastern Thrace until his death in an accident in 1355. After Orkhan's own death in 1562, his emirate acquired a new dimension.

Until this time, this emirate had developed thanks to the conjunction of several factors: its geographical position, which placed it at some distance from the neighbouring emirates; the little interest that those emirates, preoccupied with their own problems, had shown for Ottoman activities; the favourable situation for moving on Europe; the political errors of the Greeks; and the unitarism of the

Ottoman Empire, its organisation – both administrative and military – as well as its religious motivation, which had been reinforced by the successes achieved in Europe.

Upon the death of Orkhan, the Ottomans' conquests were still limited in scope, but they held both shores of the Dardanelles and were solidly entrenched in Thrace. In Asia Minor their territory stretched to the shores of the Aegean, but they held off attacking the relatively powerful emirates of Sarukhan and Aydin, because there could be as yet no question of fighting on two fronts. The same is true for the southeast, where the emirate of Germian had escaped the covetousness of Orkhan, who was entirely occupied with the Byzantine world whose situation appeared increasingly precarious.

FROM EMIRATE TO EMPIRE (1362–1451)

Organisers, and Conquerors of Christians

Murad I (or Murat, 1362–89) is the true founder of the Ottoman power in eastern Europe. His reign was marked by the capture of Adrianople (modern Edirne) from 1363, followed by the occupation of Macedonia, eastern Thrace and Bulgaria. On several occasions, and with different outcomes, he mounted an offensive against the Serbs. It was during the last battle against them, at Kosovo (13 June 1389), that he was assassinated, but the Serbs were defeated. In Anatolia, he routed and repulsed eastward the emirs of Karaman, main rivals of the Ottomans, and acquired the borderlands of the Karamanids.

But above all, he laid the foundations of a great state. He set up a centralized administration (the *Divan*), with various offices and headed by the Grand Vizier. He created a system of recruitment for his army that drew future janissaries from among the children of Christian homes in the Balkans and sent them to Anatolia to be converted to Islam, educated in Turkish culture, and taught the art of war or, in some cases, placed in service at the palace – the latter were known as *ajemioghlan*. Control over the conquered lands was exercised by distributing larger or smaller parcels of land (known as *timar* or *zimayet*) on a personal and temporary basis to military men entrusted with their exploitation and expected to provide a certain number of auxiliary soldiers. The titles given to Murad I affirm the transformation of the Ottoman state: whereas Orkhan had borne the titles of 'emir' and 'bey', Murad in the last years of his reign called himself Sultan, a sign of higher dignity.

His son Bayezid I (Bayazid), known as Yildirim ('Thunderbolt'), annexed all the Turkish emirates of western and central Anatolia except for Karaman, and then went on to conquer the Balkans. He supported Manuel II's accession to the Byzantine throne upon the death of John V (1391), although this did not prevent him from launching the siege of Constantinople shortly thereafter. In response to the Turks' advance as far as the frontiers of Hungary between 1393 and 1395, the Hungarian king Sigismund called upon the West to begin a crusade, which Pope Boniface IX endorsed enthusiastically. French, English, German, and some Italian Crusaders joined the Hungarians to attack the Turks and chase them from Europe. The clash occurred on 25 September 1396 at Nicopolis and ended in the utter defeat of the Crusaders. This defeat had a profound impact on Europe and earned the Turks their reputation for strength and even invincibility.

Defeat at the Hands of Tamerlane

Yet this invincibility was to be challenged soon thereafter. Indeed, during the final years of the fourteenth century, a new threat faced eastern Anatolia, coming from the Mongolian troops of Tamerlane (Timur Leng), the master of Central Asia, who claimed to be a descendant of Genghis Khan, and who little by little gained control of Iran and Iraq. For his part, Bayezid had occupied the territories of northeastern Anatolia and thus found himself face to face with Tamerlane. War did not break out until 1402: on 20 July, at Ankara, Bayezid was defeated by Tamerlane and taken prisoner, along with one of his sons, while Tamerlane reconstituted the emirates that Bayezid had annexed. The Ottoman Empire thus lost all its conquests in Anatolia. Even worse, the sons of the Ottoman Sultan were fighting over his legacy, so that there followed ten years of internecine war from which Mehmed I (Mehmet) ultimately emerged victorious in 1412.

On the Asian continent, where the Karamanids had profited from the situation in order to regroup, the Ottomans had to start afresh. By contrast, their European subjects remained faithful and did not make any effort to liberate themselves. Should this be considered a sign of unconditional submission, of an acceptance of their subordination to the Ottomans that they considered bearable, or of the physical impossibility of a revolt? The question remains open.

The defeat of Ankara dealt a severe – but not decisive – blow to the Ottoman state. Furthermore, the latter had found in Mehmed I a leader capable of redressing the situation. Indeed, by the time of his death in 1421, the emirates of Anatolia had been reintegrated into the Ottoman domains, a few rebellions had been crushed, and the Hungarians once again defeated. In sum, the Ottomans did not suffer more than a temporary setback in their expansion. The latter continued again even more successfully under the new Sultan, Murad II, in both Europe and northern Anatolia. The advance of the Turks in Europe provoked a new crusade, more limited than the previous one, which also failed (Varna, 10 November 1444). However, the Hungarian leader John Hunyadi led a stubborn resistance to the Turks, while in Albania, George Kastriota (Skander Beg) led a rebellion that lasted for 20 years.

A State Between Two Maritime Powers

When Murad II died in 1451, he bequeathed to his son Mehmed II a consolidated empire, a powerful army, and an able administration, the leaders of which (the viziers) were mostly the descendants of old Turkish families. Murad I had also turned Adrianople, his capital, into an intellectual and artistic centre.

The local lords in the conquered provinces initially retained their ancient privileges and social position under the control of the Ottomans. The conqueror strove to bring as few changes as possible to their territories in either economic or social terms, and to permit daily life to continue as normally as possible – languages, religions and customs were maintained. The Ottoman state contented itself with ensuring the security of these territories, for which the latter were obliged to provide taxes and soldiers. As for the lands abandoned by their former owners, the Sultan distributed them in the form of *timar* and *ziyamet* to military or civilian functionaries as a form of reward. This *timar* system was to expand gradually in a subsequent phase, as the native landlords were assimilated, 'Turkified', or disappeared. But the local populations continued to preserve their particularities. Thus, little by little the Ottoman state was organized. It still lacked a great capital, however – Mehmed II was to create one.

There was nevertheless one area in which the Ottomans were not able to overcome the superiority of the West – namely, at sea, where the Genoans and above all the Venetians were supreme masters. The Genoans concluded a series of local accords with the Turks that allowed them to engage in trade with the Ottomans from places like Phocaea, for example, and from certain Black Sea ports. The Venetians protected their empire of Romania, and even if they participated to a limited degree in anti-Turkish ventures, they strove to maintain good relations with the Ottomans while pretending to give the Byzantines aid, although this was generally too little too late. Until the mid-fifteenth century, as long as their colonies were not directly threatened, the Venetians often played a double – or even triple – game, the goal of which was to protect their territorial advantages, local privileges and commercial activities.

THE ZENITH OF THE EMPIRE

The Ottoman Empire's period of splendour lasted from the accession of Mehmed II (1451) to the end of the reign of

Süleyman the Magnificent (1566). During this century, Turkish supremacy extended over the entire Balkans, part of central Europe, the Arab Near East, and North Africa (with the exception of Morocco). Even the high seas were ruled by Ottoman corsairs. These hundred or so years also saw remarkable intellectual and especially artistic activity, with the construction of the great mosques of the Sultans. Most significantly, the Sultan controlled all trade, from the Indian Ocean by way of the Red Sea or the (Persian/Arabian) Gulf, that passed through the Arabian isthmus on the way to the Mediterranean in order to reach the capital or western Europe, since the trade route via the Cape of Good Hope had not yet become a serious rival. This commercial domination provided the Empire with enormous resources over and above the revenues gained from conquests of territory.

The Conquest of a Capital: Istanbul

The first great success of this period was the capture of Constantinople by Mehmed II (thenceforth known as Fatih, 'Conqueror') on 29 May 1453, after a siege lasting a month and a half. The taking of the city provided the Turkish Sultan with the missing link between Europe and Asia, and made him heir to the Byzantine emperors. In religious terms, the victory appeared to signify divine blessing upon the victory of Islam over Christendom. Constantinople – later known as Istanbul – became the capital of a more and more formidable empire: the dynasties of eastern Europe and the Aegean became its vassals, and the Genoese and Venetians hurried to conclude trade agreements and even peace treaties with it.

The fall of Constantinople had wide-ranging repercussions in Europe, but did not elicit any immediate reaction except to reinforce the idea of an invincible Turkish power, destroyer of Christian and Greek civilizations. The latter notion was far from the truth, for even though the Ottoman state had an excellent administration following well-defined procedures, as the organic laws (*kânûn-nâme*) passed at the time attest, it also preserved local customs and traditions. Moreover, a Sultan like Mehmed II the Conqueror was an empire-builder, an enlightened sovereign – though sometimes cruel – and a highly literate man. As soon as he was installed in his new capital, Constantinople, during the winter of 1457-58, he made it into one of the pillars of the Islamic world as well as a centre of intellectual and artistic life where Christians and Muslims worked side by side.

During his reign (1451-81), the Ottomans extended their Empire over the Peloponnese, Albania, Bosnia and Moldavia. In Anatolia, the emirate of Karaman was definitively incorporated into the Empire (1474). On the Black Sea, the Crimean khanate came under Ottoman sovereignty, and the Genoese lost Caffa and Azov as well as Lesbos in the Aegean Sea. After a war between Turkey and Venice, both sides signed a peace treaty in 1479 allowing the Venetians to retain their possessions and commercial privileges – but obliging them for the first time to pay an annual tribute of 100,000 ducats.

Bayezid II (1481-1512), following a struggle against his brother Jem, entered an unsuccessful conflict with the Mamluks (Mamelukes) of Egypt, and then with the Venetians, who lost their territories in the Peloponnese (1502), and with the Hungarians (treaty of 1505). The last years of the reign of Bayezid II were marked by the development of Turkish administration and especially, from 1509, by the rebellions of his son Selim, who with the help of janissaries defeated his father and forced him to abdicate. Under Mehmed II and Bayezid II, a systematic policy of Turkish settlement had been implemented in Constantinople and the Balkans – but in Constantinople, non-Turks and non-Muslims were also brought in, both as volunteers and compulsorily, in order to give the city the appearance and vigour worthy of a great capital.

The Sultans, Protectors of the Holy Cities

With Selim I (1512-21), the Ottoman Empire entered its most glorious period. It began with an attack, on an insignificant pretext, against Iran's sovereign, Shah Ismaïl, a troublesome neighbour considered to be religiously heterodox. In 1514, Shah Ismaïl was defeated: eastern Anatolia and Azerbaijan fell into Turkish hands. Then in 1515 it was Cilicia and Kurdistan that were conquered, as a prelude to the offensive against the Mamluks of Egypt and Syria. In 1516, following a victory over the Mamluk Sultan in Marj-Dabiq, both Syria and Palestine (August-November) were defeated. On 22 January 1517 the battle of Mount Mokattam near Cairo crowned the Mamluks' defeat and the incorporation of Egypt into the Ottoman Empire. Selim received the homage as well of the Sheriff of Mecca and was officially recognized as the 'protector and servant of the two holy cities'.

The last Abbasid Caliph, al-Mutawakkil, the spiritual leader of Sunni Islam based in Cairo, played only a very modest political role, but as the successor to the Prophet nevertheless continued to command the faithful. Selim transferred him to Constantinople. Did the Caliph – who returned to Cairo after Selim's death – ever renounce the caliphate in favour of the latter? No one knows – yet it was only in the eighteenth century (and thereafter until 1924) that the Ottoman Sultans officially bore the title of Caliph, at a time when their authority began to be challenged. Until then they do not seem to have felt the need to proclaim themselves Caliphs: the reality of their supremacy over the Sunni Muslim world was sufficiently assured for them to be able to do without that status.

The son and successor of Selim I is known in the Orient under the name Kanuni Süleyman (Süleyman the Lawgiver) and in the West as Süleyman the Magnificent. These two qualifiers illustrate perfectly the essential aspects of the work of this extraordinary person, the greatest Sultan of the dynasty, who reigned from 1521 to 1566. His conquests brought almost all Arab areas under Ottoman rule. Iraq, Arabia, and North Africa (except for Morocco) recognized its sovereignty directly or, sometimes, indirectly. The Christian powers surrendered Belgrade, Rhodes, a large part of Hungary, and Transylvania. Campaigning against Emperor Charles V in central Europe, the Mediterranean, and North Africa, Süleyman went as far as besieging Vienna (September-October 1529), spreading terror through a large part of Europe, where he challenged the emperor's hegemony, while the king of France, Francis I, sought to enter into an alliance with him. His rule on earth was matched by his supremacy at sea, where Süleyman's navy – which included many privateers – ruled the eastern Mediterranean and, after a series of victorious incursions into the western Mediterranean, successfully incorporated into the Empire several 'barbarian countries' (Algeria, Tunisia, Tripolitania) and contributed to keeping the Spanish navy at a safe distance from the vital regions of Anatolia, the Balkans and Egypt.

A Centralised Administration and a Strong Army

More than ever, the Ottoman Sultan was at this time an absolute monarch, the temporal and spiritual ruler of the Empire. When he was not participating in military expeditions, he resided in Constantinople at the palace built on Seraglio Point, or else at Adrianople. It was at the palace that the meetings of the *Divan* (government council) were held and that the family and servants of the Sultan (the harem, comprising several thousand persons) were housed. The government was the responsibility of the Grand Vizier, assisted by a number of viziers whose powers could be revoked at any time, by two military judges (*kadi-asker*), the chancellor (*nichanji*), the state treasurer (*defterdar*), the lord admiral (*kapudan pasha*) and the *agha* of the janissaries.

The state's revenues consisted of fixed and proportional taxes levied on the lands of its tributaries, tithes collected from the lands of Muslims, poll taxes imposed upon non-Muslims, customs revenues, and special taxes. To this must be added local payments, inheritance duties, tributes paid by certain provinces (Egypt, Iraq) and by the 'protected states' (Walachia, Moldavia, Ragusa). All these revenues, mainly in the form of rents, were recorded in registers that were updated regularly.

The army, reorganized on several occasions, took definitive shape in the early sixteenth century. Comprising troops appointed by the Treasury, there were janissaries, gunners, armourers, supply trains, cavalry (*sipahi*), troops from the provinces provided by the holders of *timar* and *ziyamet* lands, and irregular troops. The bulk of the army came from among the janissaries, whose recruitment was assured by the conscription of young Christians (*devshirme*). Until the sixteenth century they were forbidden to marry, but then, under Selim II or Murad III, this prohibition was dropped and recruitment became less strict – the janissaries were even permitted to have sources of revenue apart from their military service. From that time onward corruption appeared, revolts multiplied, and the Turkish army ceased to be the formidable corps it had once been. Its artillery had long been the best in Europe, but after the sixteenth century the Sultans failed to modernize it or adapt it to the innovations of the West, until by the eighteenth century the army was obliged to seek the assistance of a French engineer, Baron de Tott, to reorganize it.

By contrast, the navy – to a large degree made up of privateers – was one of the essential elements of Turkish supremacy. Despite the heavy defeat suffered at Lepanto (1571), it was thanks to its excellence that Tunis and La Goulette were taken in 1574. The fleet had arsenals based in the Mediterranean and the Black Sea, the most important of which was at Constantinople.

The Empire was thus both well defended and well administered, especially since regulations governing life in the provinces were regularly examined, revised, and adapted to new conditions, thus avoiding any harm to the inhabitants. Economic life was carefully controlled: the various trade bodies, whose activities were subject to regulation, were supervised by the *muhtesib*, assistant to the *kadi*. Regular provisioning of Constantinople also had to be assured, as did supply lines for the army. And in the provinces, local authorities had to enforce the regulations that had been decreed centrally.

A Rich and Prosperous Civilization

As regards foreign trade, the Venetians and Genoese had their privileges renewed regularly or when circumstances warranted, but their position was much less strong at the end of the sixteenth century than it had been under the Byzantines, although Venice still held pride of place among the nations trading with the Ottoman Empire. In the course of the sixteenth century, other western countries joined their ranks, France chief among them, thanks to the advantages gained under the concessions of 1535, renewed several times in the sixteenth and seventeenth centuries. French merchants enjoyed establishment privileges in the ports of the Levant, rights to fly the flag on their ships, and considerable customs exemptions. Consulates were established in various places throughout the empire: Syrian Tripoli, Aleppo, Alexandria, etc.

Other European states in turn gained similar concessions: the English in 1579, the Dutch in 1612. Commercial companies were founded to export western manufactured goods to the Ottoman Empire, especially cloth, and to bring back spices and less often wheat, trade in which was strictly controlled. The end of the sixteenth century and especially the seventeenth saw the emergence of the trade patterns that would gradually be transformed into the exploitation of the Ottoman Empire's resources for European industry, the finished products of which were destined for sale in the Empire's markets. This situation was the result of the industrial progress made by the West, and the failure of the East to adapt, for a variety of reasons, to the transformations occurring in this domain. Finally, the competition represented by the Cape route for trade in products from the Far East and Central Africa became significant from the end of the sixteenth century.

As far as artistic and intellectual life was concerned, the sixteenth century was the Ottoman golden age – an era of masterpieces in literature and, especially, art. In the field of literature, the science of history held pride of place, in terms both of Ottoman history and of chronicles of world events. Poetry was also held in high esteem. Some of the Sultans were good poets themselves, but it is the names of Fuzuli and Baki that enjoy the highest literary reputation. Art was linked to the grandeur and wealth of the Empire, thanks to its enormous revenues and capacity to recruit manpower in Iran, Syria and Egypt. From the end of the fifteenth century, the first great mosques of the Sultans began to appear, inspired by the basilica of Hagia Sophia. In the sixteenth century, the Ottoman art forms were coordinated by an architect of genius, Sinan, who adapted the internal design of Hagia Sophia to that of a mosque, giving it a new style, both original and distinctive, that would spread to all the provinces of the Empire.

The most beautiful works of Sinan are the Shehzade Mosque (1548), the mosque of Süleyman the Magnificent (Süleymaniye, 1550-57) in Constantinople, and the mosque of Selim (1564-74) at Adrianople. In addition, a number of monuments were decorated with splendidly-coloured faience made in the workshops of the Golden Horn, Nicaea and Rhodes.

THE BEGINNING OF THE END (1570-1774)

The sovereigns who succeeded Süleyman the Magnificent – Selim II and Murad III – had nothing like his personality. Their reigns were marked less by the absolute nature of their power than by their anxiety to satisfy their whims, to which their successors in turn were even more enslaved.

Rebellions and Anarchy (Seventeenth Century)

The end of the sixteenth century did see several successes – the conquest of Cyprus (1570-71), the capture of Tunis (1574), and the occupation of Georgia and Azerbaijan (1590). But the Empire also suffered defeats at Lepanto (7 October 1571), and in Moldavia and Hungary. The treaties concluded during this period brought few actual modifications to the boundaries apart from a few expansions to the east. Ahmed I (1604-17), known mainly for having built the Blue Mosque of Istanbul, had to face revolts in various parts of the Empire, the first indication of the disintegration that would become much more evident with the janissaries' murder of Sultan Osman II (May 1622), a young monarch keen to renew the Empire.

During the next few years, *de facto* power was exercised by Keussem (Kösem) Sultana, the mother of the heir, Murad IV. And after a few years of disorder Murad IV assumed governance of the Empire. Thereupon, the Sultans once again fought over power, the administration fell apart, the army rebelled, and the economic situation deteriorated. The Empire was on the edge of ruin when a Grand Vizier, Mehmed Keuprulu (Mehmet Köprülü, in September 1656), decided to take a strong hand and restore order, sparing no one. Upon his death in 1661, the work of restoration was on track.

It was carried forward by his son Ahmed, who undertook the last Ottoman conquest – that of the island of Crete, begun in 1645 and completed in 1669. After him, Kara Mustafa Pasha and two other Keuprulu – Huseyin and Numan – could strive only to limit the damage done, especially abroad, for after the failure of the second siege of Vienna (1683) the Turks were defeated on several other occasions. The Treaty of Karlowitz (28 January 1699) is the first unfavourable peace treaty signed by the Ottomans, by which they lost almost all their lands in Hungary, while the Venetians, Poles and Russians, in alliance with the Austrians, obtained several territorial advantages.

This was also the first time that the Russians became full players on the Ottoman stage. To be sure, during the seventeenth century they had made significant gains – they occupied the Ukraine and, having become neighbours to the Turks, undertook incursions into Ottoman territory. Peter the Great was recognized as Tsar by the Turks, installed an Orthodox patriarchate in Moscow and sought to gain the right to protect Orthodox Christians within the Ottoman Empire. The latter plan failed, primarily because a new Russo-Turkish War, brought about by the intrigues of King Charles XII of Sweden, led to the defeat of the Russians and the loss of all the advantages they had acquired since 1699 (the Treaty of Adrianople, 1713).

The Russian Advance (1713-74)

If the Turks had hitherto more or less succeeded in containing their adversaries, in the course of the eighteenth century they signed a string of disadvantageous treaties such as the Treaty of Passarowitz, which embodied the triumph of the Austrians (July 1718), a victory that would be attenuated somewhat by the peace of Belgrade (1739). To the east, the Ottomans were obliged to hand over the provinces of the Caucasus to the Persians (1936). Later, another Russo-Turkish War, declared following a Russian attack on Poland (a country guaranteed by the Ottomans), ended in the destruction of the Turkish navy at Chechme near Smyrna (modern Izmir), and in the invasion of Walachia. The Treaty of Kuchuk-Kainarji (21 July 1774) confirmed the Russians' access to the Black Sea and granted them freedom of navigation there and the right to cross the straits with their merchant fleet. For their part the Ottomans recovered the territories occupied by the Russians in Walachia and Bessarabia.

The Treaty of Kuchuk-Kainarji is considered to be the starting-point for the 'Eastern question'. Until then neither the French nor the English, nor even the Dutch, had reacted to the Russian advance: they were too preoccupied with their own conflicts and the conquest of colonies or of commercial markets in Asia and Africa. During the seventeenth century, the English and the Dutch developed their trade in the Ottoman Empire considerably, supplanting the French. In the second half of the eighteenth century, the French returned to the fore – but this was actually because their rivals were becoming more interested in the Americas, India and the Far East. The English, masters of India at the end of the eighteenth century, would not fail to respond to a Russian expansion that might threaten, if not their empire in Asia, then at least the route to India. The diplomatic encounters and military clashes between the English and the Russians, as well as between the Austrians and the French, would henceforth pass through the Ottoman Empire, which became the disputed terrain at stake in the 'Eastern question'.

THE 'EASTERN QUESTION' (1774-1878)

Reforms in an Empire in Crisis

When Sultan Selim III came to power (April 1789), the Ottoman Empire was once again at war with the Russians and the Austrians. The Treaty of Svishtov (August 1791) with Austria was to mark the end of hostilities for about a century and preserve the status quo concerning the borders. However, the Empire was obliged to surrender further territories to Russia under the Treaty of Jassy (January 1792). At this point Selim III wanted to introduce reforms in the Empire, especially within the army. The promulgation of the *Nizam-i cedid* (new order, 1793) was one element of these, but proved insufficient because it did not significantly reform the janissary corps, which had all too often been the source of trouble. At the same time, rebellions broke out in several provinces: Syria, Hejaz, Bulgaria and Serbia. Furthermore, Bonaparte's expedition in Egypt at this time provoked a serious crisis in Turkish-French relations (1798-1802). When Selim III once again sought to reorganize the army, the janissaries revolted, marched on Constantinople, and deposed the Sultan, who was executed shortly thereafter (June 1808). Mustafa IV, Sultan for only a few weeks, was succeeded by Mahmud II (Mahmut, 1808-39), who was to initiate numerous reforms.

Having signed the Treaty of Bucharest with the Russians (May 1812) granting them Bessarabia and recogniszing a certain degree of Serbian autonomy, Mahmud II undertook a gradual series of reforms, of which the major one was the suppression and massacre of the janissaries in June 1826. But these reforms were still limited in scope. They were to be continued and expanded by Sultan Abdul-Majid (Abdülmecit) who, by the promulgation of the *hatt-i sherif* (august edict) of Gül-Hane (3 November 1839), was to inaugurate the real period of reforms, the *Tanzimat*.

This edict decreed that all (male) subjects of the Empire are equal, without distinction of religion or nationality, that the law is the same for everyone, that every man shall pay taxes directly to the state in proportion to his fortune, and that military service would be instituted and decided by drawing lots. Reforms were also introduced into traditional education. They were not to be implemented effectively until the reign of Sultan Abdul-Aziz (Abdülaziz, 1861–76). The central authority was organized on the European model, with ministerial departments and ministers responsible for each. In May 1868 a Council of State and a Supreme Court of Justice were created, both composed of Muslims and Christians. Finally, it is important to note the appearance of newspapers: first official ones, and then private ones.

All these reforms took place at a time when the Empire was shaken by grave crises, in particular by uprisings of a nationalist character – in Serbia, which after 15 years of struggle was able to gain recognition as an autonomous principality under Turkish sovereignty; in Epirus, where Ali of Tepedelen (or Tebelen) resisted the Ottomans for 20 years (1803–22); in Egypt, where Mehmed Ali (Muhammad Ali) had himself declared governor (1805), liquidated the feudal and military regime of the Mamluks (1811), and then imposed his authority over Hejaz (1812), the Wahhabis of Arabia (1818) and the Sudan (1821).

The Emancipation of Egypt and Greece (1797–1830)

The two most serious crises occurred, in short succession, over Greece and Egypt. The idealistic liberation movement launched by Rhigas Pheraios in 1779 was followed in 1821 by a national insurrection aimed at obtaining the unconditional independence of Greece. This insurrection was strongly supported by Tsar Nicholas I, somewhat more weakly by the British, who did not particularly wish to favour Russian involvement, and by the French, who were on good terms with the Ottomans. The latter launched an appeal for intervention by the Egyptian troops of Mehmed Ali, who was occupying Crete and later took Morea (1822–25). When in March 1826 the Treaty of Akkerman in the Ukraine gained Nicholas I important concessions from the Turks, Britain reacted and called for international mediation, but the

Sultan would not accept this proposed solution. A conflict resulted that was to see the destruction of the Ottoman navy at Navarino (October 1827). After a significant advance by the Russians through eastern Anatolia and Thrace, the conflict ended with the Treaty of Adrianople (September 1829) and the London Conference (February 1830). Greece was declared independent and the Russians obtained Podolia. Serbia, Moldavia and Walachia became autonomous. The Straits were opened up to all merchant shipping.

The Greek crisis had hardly been resolved when the Egyptian crisis began. Mehmed Ali, unhappy about the Sultan's ingratitude towards him, invaded Syria, Lebanon, and even a part of Anatolia. Once again the Russians intervened, and by the Treaty of Hünkar-Iskelessi (8 July 1833) obtained important military privileges, while by the Treaty of Kutahya (May 1933) the Sultan yielded Cilicia and Syria to Mehmed Ali. These treaties satisfied no one and the hostilities resumed. The British (who occupied Aden in 1839) and the Russians intervened diplomatically on behalf of the Sultan, and the French on the side of the Egyptians. Finally, in November 1940 Mehmed Ali renounced Syria, but was recognized as hereditary leader of Egypt. As for the British, through the Convention of the Straits they succeeded in achieving the closure of the Bosporus and the Dardanelles to all non-Turkish warships.

The Dismemberment of the Empire (1840-78)

After about a decade of peace, in the course of which the reforms of 1839 were implemented, difficulties emerged with regard to the holy sites, which were then under the protection of the Russians but were claimed by the French under the terms of the concessions that had been made. The disagreement degenerated into war as a result of the Russian demands. The siege of Sebastopol (1854-55) was the key episode in the subsequent Crimean War, which ended with the Treaty of Paris (30 March 1856) and the promulgation of a new edict of reforms by the Sultan (*hatt-i hümayun* of February 1856). Another result of this treaty was the union of

Moldavia and Walachia, which in 1862 merged to form Romania. Around the same time, a local insurrection led to the granting of a special status to Lebanon (1861-64).

The following years were marked by a power struggle between the French and the British, waged in Cairo and Constantinople. The French won out and saw their efforts crowned with the grand inauguration of the Suez Canal on 17 November 1869, a ceremony in which Sultan Abdul-Aziz took part. Shortly before then, an insurrection in Crete had led to the promulgation of a statute placing the island under a mixed Christian and Muslim administration. Then around 1870 several incidents occurred in Bulgaria, Serbia, Bosnia and Romania, in which Russia was also mixed up. Despite western attempts to mediate, and in spite of the liberalization of the Ottoman regime under Sultan Abdul-Hamid II (Abdülhamid, 1876), the rise to power of a group of liberals under Midhat Pasha, and the enactment of a constitution (December 1876), war broke out, first between the Serbs and the Turks, and then between the Russians and the Turks.

Despite a valiant defence, the Turks were defeated and obliged to sign the peace treaty of San Stefano (3 March 1878), which sealed the triumph of Russia and its hegemony over the Balkans. But in face of the anxieties of Britain and Austria, Bismarck intervened and convened the Congress of Berlin (June 1878), which constituted a new stage in the dismemberment of the Ottoman Empire. Serbia and Romania became fully independent states; a new autonomous province, Eastern Rumelia, was created to the north of Rodhópis, populated by Bulgarians; Greece annexed Thessaly and part of Epirus; and Austria was able to occupy Bosnia and Herzegovina. As for Russia, it obtained the regions of Kars, Ardahan and Batum. Macedonia received a status comparable to that of Crete. In return for its alliance with Turkey, Britain was given the island of Cyprus, and through a series of secret agreements Britain, France and Italy divided up North Africa in advance, from Tunisia to Egypt. From this moment on, the Ottoman Empire might well be described as the 'sick man' of Europe.

FROM THE OTTOMAN EMPIRE TO THE TURKISH REPUBLIC

Abdul-Hamid II and the Reaction (1878-1908)

Abdul-Hamid II, brought to power by a reformist and liberal wave, did not long follow this path. A little over a year after the constitution was promulgated, he suspended it and prorogued Parliament *sine die* (February 1878). Hostile to the innovators and embittered by the concessions wrested by the West, he re-established absolute power and based his political programme on pan-Islamism in the hope of reuniting around himself all the Muslims of the Empire, making minority groups into scapegoats if necessary. The Armenians in particular were the victims of this policy (massacres in 1894 and 1896). Yet this approach did not succeed in restoring political or economic stability.

For the Ottoman Empire was going through a dramatic financial crisis at the time. It was able to guarantee public services only thanks to advances granted by the Ottoman Bank (an Anglo-French bank founded in 1863). By the Decree of Muharrem (20 December 1881), the Bank was able to make up for the state's default through collecting important revenues, administered by a new organization: the Ottoman Public Debt Administration. Under the title of the Imperial Ottoman Bank, this body became the official state bank, even while continuing to be a foreign-owned company. Several British, French, German, Austrian and Belgian enterprises were given the right to provide key services, exploit resources, and build roads and railways, and were granted enormous special advantages.

The rivalry among the great powers went beyond the economic field and spilled over into the political, especially after the Germans obtained the Baghdad railway concession and the right to participate in the research and development of oil deposits (Turkish Petroleum Company). This particularly alarmed Britain, anxious to protect the route to India in the face of the German *Drang nach Osten*. Moreover, since the discovery of Iranian oil fields, the British had been anxious to secure a monopoly over oil in the East.

In addition to these economic difficulties came political problems: in Crete, where an insurrection provoked a Greco-Turkish war (1897), and in Bulgaria, where the Russians tried to impose their rule and where the question of Macedonia arose (1897-1903). In essence, the entire 'Balkan question' was the result of the rivalries among Turks, Bulgarians, Greeks and Serbs in connection with this province.

The Young Turks and the Invasion of the Ottoman Lands (1908-19)

It was under these circumstances that the revolution of the 'Young Turks', who led the Committee of Union and Progress, broke out. Intellectuals and Ottoman officers, liberals and reformers, living either within the borders of the Empire or in exile, sought to reconstruct a liberal state that would be able to throw off the European stranglehold. A first uprising, in July 1908, provoked by the officers of Salonica, forced the Sultan to restore the constitution of 1876. A wave of enthusiasm swept through the Empire, and the Arab provinces adhered more closely to the new government. But that government, as a result of the foreign policy situation, was obliged to abandon its liberal line and follow a more authoritarian approach based on pan-Turkism, thus alienating in one stroke the sympathy of the Arabs and of minority groups.

War continued interminably to rage in the last remaining Ottoman territories. In Africa, after the loss of Tunisia – occupied by France in 1881 – Tripolitania was next to fall, when the Italians landed there in 1911. The Italians also conquered Rhodes and the Dodecanese – conquests that were recognized by the Treaty of Ouchy (October 1912). Then came the first Balkan War, in which Bulgarian, Greek and Serb allies attacked the Turks, ending in the loss of almost all of Thrace (December 1912). However, disagreement among these allies over the division of the conquered territory allowed the Turks, in the course of the second Balkan War, to recover Adrianople, eastern Thrace, and the islands of Tenedos and Imbros (December 1913). In Constantinople the Young Turk government, after the assassination of the Grand Vizier Mahmud Chevket, further reinforced its authoritarian policies under the triumvirate of Mehmed Talât, Ahmed Jemal and Ismail Enver, and continued to rely upon German support. This was ultimately to lead it to enter World War I on the side of Germany (31 October 1914).

To the west, the French and the British failed in their attempt to cross the Dardanelles. To the east, the Russians won a series of victories that were cut short only by the Revolution of 1917. In the Arab world, the British succeeded, with some difficulty, in extending their reach as far as Baghdad (March 1917). In Arabia, Palestine and Syria they supported the Arab revolt that between 1916 and 1918 obliged the Turks to abandon those provinces. The Armistice of Mudros (30 October 1918) confirmed the Turkish defeat and led to the occupation of the borders of Anatolia by the Allies (including the Greeks), who arrived in the region of Smyrna in May 1919.

The Turkish Republic of Mustafa Kemal

The government in Constantinople could do nothing to stop the dismemberment not only of what remained of the Empire but even of Anatolia itself. One Turkish officer rose up against this dismemberment: Mustafa Kemal, who had fought in the Dardanelles and in the Near East. Beginning on 19 May 1919, he organized the struggle for the integrity and the independence of Turkey. His energy and prestige won him the support of the Anatolian population and of a certain number of politicians. This made it possible for him to reject the Treaty of Sèvres, which enshrined the dismemberment of the Empire, reduced Turkey to the Anatolian plateau alone, and envisaged the creation of an Armenian and a Kurdish state.

Between 1920 and 1922 Mustafa Kemal waged an unrelenting war of independence against the Greeks, who enjoyed the support of the British, while Kemal himself received the official backing of the Soviet Union authorities and the unofficial aid of the French and the Italians. His victories at Sakarya and Inönu led to the eviction of the Greek population of Anatolia. The peace negotiations begun after the Armistice of Mudanya (11 October 1922) were concluded by the Treaty of Lausanne (24 July 1923). The Turks recovered their former borders in Thrace and the islands of Imbros and Tenedos; the Greeks of Anatolia and the Turks of Greece were to be exchanged; and the Turks retained control of the Straits. The earlier capitulations were abrogated and there was no longer any question of forming an Armenian or a Kurdish state. The Turks for their part recognized the independence of the ancient Arab provinces.

Thus the new Turkey was born. But it still required to be given other structures. The Turkish nationalists could not countenance a return to the imperial regime, which they accused of having caused the Empire's decline. And so on 20 October 1923 the Turkish Republic was proclaimed, and as a consequence, the sultanate and the Empire disappeared. Mustafa Kemal was elected President of the Republic. In order to break even more fully with the old regime, the capital was moved to Ankara. As the last stage of the Turkish revolution, on 3 March 1924 the caliphate was abolished and the last Ottoman Caliph left for exile. Thus ended six centuries of Ottoman history, and the history of Turkey began.

MUSTAFA KEMAL ATATÜRK
ROBERT MANTRAN

Founder and first president of the Turkish Republic, Atatürk (Mustafa Kemal) was born at Salonica (modern Thessaloníki) in 1881 and died at Istanbul on 10 November 1938. He was one of the first heads of state to understand the necessity of westernizing Muslim countries. Atatürk was undoubtedly one of the most prestigious politicians of the interwar period. Some have accused him of imposing a dictatorship on Turkey. In fact, his personality towered over a presidential form of government, and he was successful in gaining the loyalty of a population aware of the progress made by Turkey under his presidency. Nevertheless, Atatürk died too soon, and was not able to bring to completion all the reforms he had envisaged. After World War II some leaders in the Muslim world were inspired by his example, and thus evidently considered him an important precursor. For the Turks, he was a man whom they referred to after his death as the 'eternal leader'.

RISE TO POWER

Having lost his father, Ali Riza (a former civil servant, later soldier, and finally a merchant), while still a child, the young Mustafa was brought up by his mother, Zübeyde Hanim. He attended primary school and then the state grammar school of Salonica before entering the military preparatory school of Salonica at the age of 12, where one of his teachers got him to add the name Kemal to that of Mustafa. In 1895 he entered the military secondary school of Monastir, and in 1899 the War College of Istanbul. Finally he attended the Military Academy, from which he graduated in January 1905 with the rank of captain.

During his time in Istanbul he began to be interested in politics, siding with the opponents of the despotic regime of Sultan Abdul-Hamid II. Upon leaving the Military Academy he was sent to Damascus, where with a few comrades he founded a secret group, *Vatan ve Hürriyet* (Homeland and Liberty). Appointed in September 1907 to the army general staff of Salonica, he devoted himself to various military tasks. In spite of the turmoil within the Ottoman Empire in 1908–09 (the deposing of Sultan Abdul-Hamid and the rise to power of the Young Turks), he insisted that the army must remain above politics. In fact, he took part only from afar in the activities of the Committee of *Ittihâd ve Terakkî* (Union and Progress). This attitude must be seen as a reflection of his opposition to some of the Young Turk leaders, especially Enver Pasha.

In 1911–12 he participated in the defence of Tripolitania against the Italian invasion, and was appointed military attaché to Bulgaria in October 1913. Because the Ottoman Empire entered World War I alongside Germany, the British and the French launched violent attacks in order to capture the Gallipoli peninsula. Mustafa Kemal, promoted colonel in June 1915, played a key role in ensuring the failure of these attacks (1915). He then commanded an army corps on the Caucasus front and recaptured the towns of Bitlis and Mus from the Russians (August 1916). It was there that he first met Colonel Ismet Pasha (the future Ismet Inönü) who was to become his most faithful companion.

Named commander of the Seventh Army in Palestine, he disagreed with the German General Falkenhayn concerning the conduct of operations, and tendered his resignation. It was refused, but he was given leave, during which he accompanied Prince Vahideddin to Germany. When, upon the death of Sultan Mehmed V, Vahideddin ascended to the throne (3 July 1918), the latter summoned Mustafa Kemal back to command the Seventh Army, with which he carried out an orderly retreat from Palestine to the north of Aleppo. It was there that he learned of the signing of the Armistice of Mudros (30 October 1918) and voiced his opposition to the clauses of the armistice, particularly those concerning the armies that he had commanded on the Syrian border.

The army units of the south having been dissolved, Mustafa Kemal returned to Istanbul, where he tried to bring about the creation of a cabinet determined to fight for the national ideals of Turkey (November 1918). However, his efforts met with opposition from Sultan Mehmed VI and the leading classes of Istanbul. He thus concluded that no action was possible except in Anatolia. It was at this time that he was appointed inspector of the Ninth Army in Erzurum, with full military and civilian powers over the provinces of Sivas, Trebizond, Erzurum and Van, and the district of Samsun (30 April 1919). Accompanied by a few friends and a couple of carefully chosen officers, he arrived at Samsun on 19 May 1919, resolved to do everything possible to secure Turkey's independence.

To the Istanbul government's decision to 'place Turkey under the protection of the great powers' (26 May 1919), Mustafa Kemal responded on 3 June with a circular in which he affirmed the necessity of defending the absolute independence of the state and the nation. Recalled to Istanbul, he refused to go, and on 22 June 1919 issued a proclamation in which he condemned the actions of the government, called upon the nation to fight to save the integrity and independence of the fatherland, and announced a forthcoming national congress to be held at Sivas, organized by the Association for the Defence of the Rights of the Oriental Provinces.

Mustafa Kemal felt all the more free to lead the struggle since the government had terminated his official duties, and since he had by then resigned from the army. At the preparatory Congress of Erzurum (23 July – 7 August 1919), of which he was named president, three major principles were formulated: the integrity, indivisibility, and independence of

Turkey; determined opposition to foreign occupation and intervention; and the creation of a provisional government if the central government should prove incapable of defending the independence of the fatherland.

The Congress of Sivas, which met from 4 September 1919, first of all established the regulations and programme of the Association for the Defence of the Rights of Anatolia and of Rumelia, thus extending its competence to the whole Turkish nation. The principles adopted at Erzurum were reaffirmed, and active opposition to foreign powers and to the government in Istanbul was further intensified. A representative committee headed by Mustafa Kemal was elected: on 14 September it was decided that this committee alone represented the nation. A newspaper, *Irade-i Milliye* (*The National Will*), was published and distributed in Anatolia.

An attempt at rapprochement with the new government in Istanbul led by Ali Riza Pasha ended in failure, especially after the occupation of Istanbul by the Allied troops on 16 March 1920 and the arrest of individuals who supported Mustafa Kemal. The latter then convened an assembly in Ankara composed of newly-elected representatives and parliamentary deputies from Istanbul willing to join the nationalists.

And so the first Grand National Assembly (GNA, *Büyük Millet Meclisi*) met in Ankara on 23 April 1920. This body decided that it represented the nation, that it would hold the legislative and executive powers until such time as the Sultan could freely resume his functions, and that it would delegate its powers to a Council of Ministers, the president of which would be the president of the Assembly. Mustafa Kemal was elected to this post, and the first national government was formed on 3 May 1920.

This government had immediately to take defensive measures against the troops sent by the Grand Vizier Damad Ferid Pasha to oppose the nationalists. Soon, however, hostilities ended on this front. At the same time, an armistice was concluded with the French on 30 May 1920, after a year of fighting in Cilicia. This was the first treaty signed by the GNA with a foreign power. To the east, the nationalist armies began to occupy the regions of Kars, Ardahan and Artvin, included within the borders of Turkey.

THE STRUGGLE FOR INDEPENDENCE

But the true struggle for independence began with the Greco-Turkish War declared on 22 June 1920, when the Greeks, with the consent of the Allies, launched an offensive toward the Anatolian plateau in order to impose the terms of the Treaty of Sèvres in that area. By August, the entire western part of Anatolia and Thrace were in Greek hands.

By contrast, in the east General Kâzim Karabekir won several victories over the Armenians, who signed an armistice on 18 November 1920. The treaties of Alexandropol (or Gümrü) (3 December 1920), Moscow (16 March 1921) and Kars (12 October 1921) recognized Turkey's possession of the territories of Kars and Ardahan, which had been lost in 1878. In August 1920 an accord was concluded with the Soviet government – one that would be renewed by the treaty of 16 March 1921.

While Mustafa Kemal was organizing the government on the basis of national and popular support, and when talks entered into by the government of Istanbul in view of a rapprochement failed, the Greeks moved to attack Eskishehir and Dumlupinar, but Ismet Pasha broke their offensive at Inönü (10–11 January 1921). In the course of the winter, negotiations were begun between the Allies – especially the French and the Italians, the nationalists, and the Ottoman government – in the hope of revising the Treaty of Sèvres. These talks yielded no satisfactory result, and in March 1921 hostilities began anew.

The Greeks again attacked in the direction of Eskisehir, but once again were defeated at Inönü (31 March). In July, the Greeks succeeded in taking Kütahya, Afyon Karahisar and Eskisehir, and Turkish troops were obliged to withdraw behind the Sakarya River. On 5 August the GNA appointed

Mustafa Kemal generalissimo with full powers for three months. On 25 August a battle began that was to last 22 days, after which the Greek army was forced to retreat. Following this victory, the GNA conferred on Mustafa Kemal the rank of marshal and the title *Gazi* ('Victorious'). A few days later, on 20 October 1921, the French government, represented by Franklin-Bouillon, signed an accord with the Turks effectively recognizing the nationalist government, and evacuated the occupied territories in southeastern Anatolia with the exception of the Sanjak of Alexandretta.

This accord was to have important consequences. Negotiations with the Allies in March-April 1922 were unsuccessful, and Mustafa Kemal, having seen his powers renewed for the fourth time, prepared for the final offensive. On 26 August 1922 the Greek lines were broken, and on 30 August the victory of Dumlupinar completed the initial success. On 9 September Turkish troops entered Smyrna – which was devastated by a conflagration three days later – and on 18 September the last Greek soldier left Anatolian soil. On 11 October, an armistice was signed at Mudanya, and soon thereafter Turkish troops reoccupied Thrace.

THE PROCLAMATION OF THE REPUBLIC

In preparation for the conference that was to be held in Lausanne in order to set the terms for peace, the Allies invited the nationalist government as well as the Sultan's government. To prevent the latter from participating, Mustafa Kemal had the GNA vote on 4 November 1922 to abolish the sultanate, despite the opposition of certain religious factions who regarded it as impossible to dissociate the sultanate from the caliphate. The last Ottoman government resigned and the ex-Sultan Mehmed VI left Istanbul on a British ship. His cousin Abdul-Mejid was elected Caliph.

The Lausanne Conference (21 November 1922 to 24 July 1923) ended with the signing of a peace treaty that established the border of Turkey in Thrace along the course of the Maritza, returned the islands of Imbros and Tenedos to the Turks, and required the Greeks to demilitarize the islands close to the Anatolian coast. The Greek populations of Turkey (except for those in Istanbul) and the Turks in Greece (except those in western Thrace) were to be exchanged; Italian sovereignty over the Dodecanese was recognized; the Straits could be remilitarized by the Turks in the event of war; the earlier capitulations were abrogated; and the Allies were to evacuate Istanbul six weeks after the ratification of the peace treaty (which occurred on 23 August 1923).

On 6 October 1923 Turkish troops entered Istanbul, bringing to an end the War of Independence. There was no longer any question of an independent Armenia or Kurdistan; the only remaining point of contention was the territory of Mosul, finally handed over to Iraq in June 1926 in return for a financial compensation.

The second Grand National Assembly was elected between June and August 1923, and on 9 August Mustafa Kemal founded the Republican People's Party, successor to the Association for the Defence of the Rights of the Oriental Provinces, and was elected its president. This party brought together the majority of the deputies. On 13 August Mustafa Kemal became president of the GNA, and on 29 October the Assembly proclaimed the Republic and elected Mustafa Kemal its President. It immediately appointed Ismet Inönü Prime Minister, and established the capital of the republic at Ankara. Finally, in the last stage of the political revolution, on 3 March 1924 the caliphate was abolished by a vote of the GNA, and the members of the Ottoman dynasty were expelled from Turkey.

THE CONSTRUCTION OF THE NEW TURKEY

Mustafa Kemal now devoted himself to the enormous task of constructing the new Turkey. For 15 years, until his death, his sole aim was to liberate Turkey and its inhabitants from their age-old chains and to bring them to a more advanced level of material, social and intellectual culture. To do this it was necessary to make a clean break with the past, to tear down traditions, even to shock people and overturn their received ideas. So many problems and difficulties remained that he alone could surmount, first by the sheer force of his character and his powerful personality, and then by the almost unanimous support of the population for its liberator. He also had to sustain and channel the enthusiasm born of the War of Independence – that is, to unify the nation not only around its President but also around the ideas he had proposed and carried out throughout the country by means of a single party, the Republican People's Party.

The six key principles of his party were: republicanism, nationalism, populism, statism, secularity and revolution. The single-party system prohibited any legal opposition – in fact, apart from the brief appearance of a Progressive Republican Party in 1924-25 and of a Liberal Republican Party in 1930 (temporary experiments only, authorized by Mustafa Kemal), the RPP remained at the centre of political activity in the country, especially after the congress of 1935, when the Minister of the Interior became simultaneously the secretary-general of the party, and the provincial governors served as the party's local presidents.

There was no lack of opposition, however, especially in the early days of the Turkish Republic. First it was the laws abolishing the caliphate, the suppression of the religious courts and religious schools, the laws promulgated in 1924 that provoked reactions from conservative and traditionalist elements. But Mustafa Kemal judged that the Ottoman Sultans had failed in their task and that, moreover, religion as it was then practised and especially as it was taught, with its regressive influence on public education, ought to be relegated to the status of a personal matter. Such a concept of a secular state was in fact introduced as an amendment to the constitution, passed on 9 April 1928. In the religious domain Mustafa Kemal thereafter had the GNA vote to abolish polygamy, suppress the religious brotherhoods, and ban the fez (August-November 1925). Later, in 1931, they added the requirement that the call for prayer be made in Turkish and no longer in Arabic, and that the Qur'an be read in Turkish – something that traditionalist Muslims found hard to accept. Insurrections of a religious nature broke out in 1925, and then in 1930, in western Anatolia: both were harshly suppressed.

The same is true for political uprisings in Kurdistan in 1925 and 1930. Disappointed in their nationalist aspirations, the Kurds did not welcome being integrated into the Turkish Republic. Their uprisings were followed by terrible repression, which for a long time put an end to any will to rebel. The Turkish government did its utmost to 'Turkify' the Kurds, but succeeded only partially in this effort.

The constitution, passed on 30 April 1924, bestowed legislative and executive powers upon the Grand National Assembly, elected for four years by universal suffrage (women obtained the vote in 1934). In effect, the elections were carefully prepared by the RPP, which alone ran candidates. The GNA in turn elected the President of the Republic for a four-year term, and the President together with the Council of Ministers held the executive power. Mustafa Kemal continued to be re-elected President of the Turkish Republic until his death.

THE ACHIEVEMENTS OF ATATÜRK

In domestic policy, modernization was marked, in juridical terms, by the adoption of new civil, criminal and commercial codes of law based upon the Swiss, Italian and German codes (January-February 1925) and by the introduction of mandatory civil marriage (September 1925). In public education, all teaching establishments at all levels were placed under state control. A university was founded in Ankara in addition to that of Istanbul, which was reformed and restructured. Mustafa Kemal was especially careful to provide for the training of teachers who, especially in the villages, would be the propagandists of the new Turkey; but the influence of local religious elements represented a serious obstacle to the spread of 'Kemalism'. The adoption, in November 1928, of the Latin alphabet in place of the Arabic one was in itself a minor revolution that the traditionalists did not accept without resistance, despite the advantages of the Latin alphabet for transcribing the Turkish language. In November 1934, a law was passed requiring all citizens to adopt surnames: the GNA gave Mustafa Kemal the last name Atatürk, which may be translated as 'patriarchal Turk', or as 'father of the new Turkey'.

In economic terms, the task was no less enormous: to make Turkey into a modern country and free it from economic dependence on western Europe. After having nullified the concessions that had permitted the West gradually to gain exorbitant advantages in the country, Mustafa Kemal strove to Turkify and then to nationalize the numerous foreign companies operating in Turkey at the time. The Ottoman Bank, symbol of the European domination of the Turkish economy, was reduced in 1931 to the status of a regular bank, and its functions as the state bank and bank of issue were taken over by the Merkez Bankasi (Central Bank). Agriculture was strongly encouraged; land was distributed to the peasants, and an agricultural bank was established favouring the modernization of the countryside. Its capacities were, however, too restricted in comparison with the enormous transformations that were needed, and most importantly, Mustafa Kemal was unable to eliminate the caste of powerful landowners who had opportunistically joined his side.

Mining and industry were placed under state control by means of national banks (Eti Bank, Sümer Bank), and in January 1934 a four-year plan for their development was launched. The same was done for commerce through the Commercial Bank (Ish Bankasi). Communication and transportation routes – especially the railways, which had also been nationalized – were expanded in order to allow better contacts with the most far-flung provinces. Within a few years, Mustafa Kemal had succeeded in placing the country's economy back on a solid footing, and indeed in giving it an unprecedented national dynamism.

In foreign policy, Mustafa Kemal pursued a resolutely pacifist programme aimed at establishing good relations with all the country's neighbours and with the great powers. He strove therefore to eliminate the negative consequences of the War of Independence and to show the world that the Turkish nation was there to stay. Thus all the remaining questions with Greece were resolved through the Treaty of Ankara, signed on 30 October 1930. The same became true with the Soviet Union (1928 and 1929), Bulgaria (1929), Italy (1926-32), France (1926-30), and Great Britain (1926-39). In June 1932 Turkey was admitted to the League of Nations, and in February 1934 it joined the Balkan Entente with Greece, Yugoslavia and Romania. In July 1936 the Montreux Convention gave Turkey full control of the Straits. Finally, in July 1937 Turkey signed the pact of Saadabad with Iraq, Iran and Afghanistan.

A disagreement arose with France concerning the Sanjak of Alexandretta, to which the Turks laid claim. Only after the death of Atatürk, and shortly before the outbreak of World War II, was the conflict resolved: the Sanjak was ceded to Turkey (becoming the province of Hatay) and the two countries signed a mutual assistance pact (19 October 1939).

Atatürk died on 10 November 1938, mourned by an entire nation to whom he had devoted his life and whom he had liberated from numerous forms of servitude. A temporary grave was placed in the Ethnographic Museum of Ankara, and on 10 November 1953 his body was solemnly transferred to the immense mausoleum built in his honour in Ankara. A man of intransigent character, deeply aware of the task that history had entrusted to him, Atatürk succeeded by sheer strength of will to triumph over all obstacles: to him, all that mattered was Turkey's recovery. An authoritarian, he could not bear contradiction: he was determined to eliminate outmoded forms of government and of an Islam he judged to be retrograde and responsible for the decline of the Ottoman Empire, and throughout his life he never ceased to oppose them. His rigour did at times lead to excesses, in relation to dealing both with some of his political adversaries and with ethnic minorities who had long been established in Turkey but who he deemed to be potential threats to national unity.

The policies followed by Atatürk gave birth to the ideology known as 'Kemalism', the principal elements of which are the defence of Turkish territory and, more generally, of 'Turkism' – secularism, direct or indirect state control of the principal means of production, and social progress through the modernization and westernization of Turkey. In time this ideology was to come to be no more than a vague symbol, a word often denoting many very different realities. In the end it became simply a slogan for the Turkish army when its leaders determined, in 1971 and in 1980, that the path followed by the country's political leaders was endangering the achievements of the 'eternal leader'.

THE GENESIS OF THE IDEA OF EUROPE
JEAN-BAPTISTE DUROSELLE

The word 'Europe' appeared, in its geographical sense, in the seventh century before Christ. A peninsula of Asia, Europe's eastern boundaries remain arbitrary. Its western limits are likewise open to debate as to whether or not certain islands belong to it. But these discussions about its borders would be purely academic if, over the centuries, the concept of Europe had not been charged with ideas and political passions. To speak of the 'idea of Europe' is to evoke the question whether, over and above the peoples, languages, religions and states, there is a 'greater community' that distinguishes this relatively small peninsula, surrounded by seas and oceans, from the massive continents that encircle it near and far.

The Greeks, dispersed over three continents, considered themselves to be different from the 'barbarians'. The unity of the Roman Empire was centred on the Mediterranean and not on Europe. When the Arabs invaded Spain, southern Italy and Gaul, they could have dominated the Mediterranean basin as the Romans had done. It was when the Arabs were forced to withdraw, starting with the battle of Poitiers (732) and ending with the Spanish *reconquista* (completed in the fifteenth century), that a political idea of Europe, coterminous with (western) Christendom, first came to light. For only one brief period, under the reign of Charlemagne, did a political unit coincide almost exactly with the zone of influence of the Roman Church. During the rest of the Middle Ages, the dream of unifying Europe was sustained either by the emperor or by the pope.

The appearance, from the fifteenth century, of states with a modern structure destroyed the hopes of achieving unity through religion. Thenceforth – till the end of World War II – the idea of Europe took three main forms:

- a Europe of the balance of powers, or in 'concert', that recognized the independence of states (especially the large ones), guaranteed by observing human rights and traditional rules (balance of power);

- a Europe unified by conquest – which was the aim of the two very different undertakings, those of Napoleon and of Hitler respectively; and

- a voluntarily united Europe, although the latter is still at the stage of a project and a dream.

It is only latterly, in the twentieth century, that politicians have seemed able to envisage the prospect of a concerted unification.

The end of World War II marks an absolute turning-point. The world became 'bipolar' and power was concentrated in two states, of which one was partly European and the other populated 90 per cent by European immigrants. The European 'powers', as a result of having fought each other, lost the technological and political dominance that had previously made it possible for them to conquer, over four centuries, almost the entire world. The idea of unity was no longer simply a matter for writers but had become an essential preoccupation of statesmen. Robert Schuman, Alcide de Gasperi and Konrad Adenauer, often inspired by Jean Monnet and supported by the United States in its Cold War with the Soviet Union, succeeded in creating community institutions, sometimes for all of non-Communist Europe, and on the economic level for the six western countries. The question was, would economic unification eventually lead to political union? The latter project often came up against unforeseen resistance, of which General de Gaulle, hostile to the notion of 'integration', was the pre-eminent symbol. The political problem was thus defined, but has not yet been resolved.

'GEOGRAPHICAL' EUROPE IN ANTIQUITY

Europe takes its name from a mythological personage, Europa: one of the 3,000 Oceanides, or a Phoenician princess kidnapped by Zeus, who took the form of a bull in order to seduce her. Why was her name given to a continent? Herodotus in the fifth century BC had already raised the question: 'But it is certain that the Tyrian Europa was of Asian birth, and never even set foot on the land which the Greeks now call Europe.' He nevertheless stated, philosophically, that 'we shall ourselves continue to use the names which custom sanctions' (*Histories* IV, 185).

The mystery has never been resolved. At the end of the seventh century, a contemporary of Hesiod wrote – in the poem entitled *To Pythian Apollo* – of 'those who live in rich Peloponnesus and those of Europe and all the wave-washed isles'. The word 'Europe' was evidently then used to refer to one part of continental Greece. Later it came to designate – in keeping with the geographical knowledge of the day – the entire peninsula attached to Asia, the eastern borders of which Herodotus set at Tanais (the Don). Today, Europe extends as far as the Ural Mountains. But this is an arbitrary definition, for the boundaries separating Europe from Asia are not delineated by any indisputable geographical frontier.

The Greeks

Europe, wrote Herodotus, is 'a wondrous beautiful region, rich in all kinds of cultivated trees' (VII, 5). But neither he nor any other Greek author attached any political significance to Europe. A Greek was proud of being Greek and felt superior to the other peoples, whom he or she referred to uniformly as 'barbarians'. Yet there were Greeks living in the western part of Asia Minor, the archipelagos of the Aegean Sea, present-day continental Greece, southern Italy, and southern Sicily. They had important colonies in northeastern Africa, in the western Mediterranean, and along the shores of the Black Sea. Divided politically into cities constantly at war with each other, the Greeks perceived the

Hellenic world in which they lived as a 'superior community', and various institutions – such as the Olympic Games – attest to this profound sense of unity. Aristotle believed that 'The nations inhabiting cold places and those of Europe are full of spirit, but somewhat deficient in intelligence', whereas 'the peoples of Asia are intelligent and skilful in temperament, but lack spirit... But the Greek race participates in both characters, just as it occupies the middle position geographically, for it is both spirited and intelligent' (*Politics*, VII, 7, 1327b ff.). There was thus a Greek 'pan-nationalism', but no sense of solidarity between the Greeks of Europe and other peoples inhabiting the same continent.

The Romans

It is certainly true that Rome is a European city. But the extraordinary conquests of the Romans were centred on the Mediterranean, *mare nostrum*, whose shores they had reached and outspread from the first century of the Christian era. Moreover, the Roman Empire did not cover all of Europe. According to the geographer Strabo, who wrote shortly before the Christian era, the Romans 'held almost all of Europe, except for the part located beyond the Ister [Danube] and the parts on the ocean coast between the Rhine and the Tanais [Don].' However, two great European zones were almost unknown to Rome: the Scandinavian countries – note that Strabo confuses the Baltic Sea with the ocean – and the vast northern plains between the Baltic shores and the Don. The Romans never succeeded in conquering all of what is now Germany, and it was only under Trajan (AD 98–117) that they crossed the Danube and took Dacia (Romania).

The word 'Europe' thus appears rarely in Greco-Latin literature. It is used almost exclusively by geographers, who show a certain predilection for it. Before describing the other continents, Strabo makes the following remark: 'We will commence with Europe, both because its figure is more varied and also because it is the quarter most favourable to the mental and social ennoblement of man, and produces a greater portion of comforts than the other continents' (*Geography*, II, 5, 8). Pliny the Elder, writing his *Natural History* less than a century after Strabo, imitates him: 'I shall first then speak of Europe, the foster-mother of that people which has conquered all other nations, and itself by far the most beauteous portion of the earth' (III, 1). But these are brief bursts of enthusiasm, not political opinions.

The Barbarians

The enormous Roman bureaucratic machinery imposed common institutions on the Empire. It was shattered in the third century by the first wave of barbarian invasions, then reconstructed in the fourth century in the new form of an empire divided into four parts – Diocletian's tetrarchy – that would last only until the fifth century. From 395 onwards, the eastern half of the Empire separated itself definitively from the western half. The latter fell in 476 to the barbarians.

It is true that in the sixth century, Justinian, at the height of the Byzantine Empire, was able to reconquer part of the west. His success was, however, ephemeral. Barbarian kingdoms, still unsteady and constantly shifting, were gradually established on the continent: the Franks in northern Gaul, Visigoths in Aquitaine and in Spain, Vandals in Africa, Ostrogoths in northern Italy, etc. Intellectual life declined under the rule of these vigorous but uncultivated peoples, and in the sixth century it was all but extinct outside of the monasteries of far-off Ireland.

During this troubled era, the word 'Europe' practically disappeared altogether. We see it mentioned in passing by Procopius, Justinian's historian, and that is about all. Curiously, when the influence of the Church of Rome began to spread – under the leadership of Pope Gregory the Great (590–604), who launched evangelizing missions all over the continent until it rivalled the strength of the Eastern Churches – a new phenomenon would impress upon Europeans a sense of their own distinctiveness: the Arab conquests.

A Europe Coterminous with Latin Christendom (Eighth to Fifteenth Centuries)

It was in 622 that the *hegira* took place – that is, Muhammad's flight from Mecca to Medina. This event, completely ignored by the Europeans of the day, symbolically marks the foundation of a new religion, but also the imminent conquest of an empire. In 711, Tariq forced his way past the 'pillars of Hercules', which after him would come to be known as the strait of Jabal al-Tariq (Gibraltar). Christian Spain fell. The Arabs crossed the Pyrenees and were not to be repulsed until Charles Martel stopped them at the battle of Poitiers (732). It was the Arab conquest that brought the word 'Europe' back into use, and moreover, for the first time gave it a political meaning. The English monk known as the Venerable Bede (*c*.673–735) used the word twice. More significantly, in 769, three decades after Poitiers, the Spanish Isidore of Beja, when recounting the battle, called the army of Charles Martel the army 'of the Europeans': 'Leaving their homes in the morning, the Europeans perceived the well-ordered tents of the Arabs.'

What intellectual trajectory led up to this point? We do not know. The important thing is to understand that the struggle against the Arab invaders was that of the Christians against the Muslims, and that wherever the clash occurred (Spain, Frankish Gaul, southern Italy) a new solidarity appeared in spite of internecine struggles. It was reinforced by the actions of the popes at a time when communications with the Byzantine world were much reduced.

Charlemagne

This solidarity reached its peak with the conquests of Charlemagne, the Frankish king who was crowned emperor by the pope in 800. But such solidarity was to prove ephemeral. At the beginning of Charlemagne's reign, a cleric named Cathulf suggested that he thank God for having given him domination over 'Europe'. In 799, the poet Angilbert called him 'venerable leader of Europe' and 'king, father of Europe': 'Charles, learned, modest ... master of the world, beloved of his people ... the pinnacle of Europe ... is in the process of redrawing the walls of the new Rome.' At this time the idea of Europe more or less coincided with that of the new Rome – that is to say, the reconstituted Western Empire. Charlemagne, blessed and crowned by the pope, wielded a decisive influence over the pontiff. 'Europe' in this period meant Gaul, non-Muslim Spain, the Low Countries, Germany and Italy, where Charlemagne had triumphed over the Lombards. The Empire was coterminous with the present-day countries of the common market, not including the Roman Church's mission fields. But it was clearly distinct from the Eastern Empire. Indeed, in 863 the Eastern and Western Churches split apart (the definitive schism occurred in 1058).

Charlemagne's empire did not survive him for long. The territory was divided up by the Treaty of Verdun in 843. The empire of the Ottonians in the tenth and eleventh centuries would be of much more modest dimensions, although this did not stop the author of the *Annals of Quedlinburg*, describing the coronation of Otto III in 996, from writing with some hyperbole: 'This enthronement, performed by the Apostolic See, crowned our lord Otto, hitherto known as king, as august emperor, to the acclamation not only of the Roman people but of the peoples of all Europe.'

The Dream of the Middle Ages: the Restoration of Unity

Thenceforward, Charlemagne was a leader of legendary proportions. In the highly complex history of the Middle Ages, where authority was continually fragmented, there were never-ending plans for union – the work of intellectuals and partisans. Initially, the word 'Europe' once again became rare. Charlemagne's empire was, according to the historian Nithard (d. 858), *tota occidentalis Europa*. The word *occidentalis* soon disappeared, as did the word *Europa*, replaced by the term *Christianitas*, Christendom. But who would govern Christendom – the pope or the emperor? The struggle raged for several centuries, beginning in earnest with the papcy of Gregory VII (1073–85), between the partisans of the *sacerdotium* – who placed the pope above the emperor and other temporal princes – and those of the *regnum* – who reserved all temporal power to the emperor. Thus there were two ways of conceiving of unity, which alone would make it possible to carry out the enormous task of the Crusades and the *Reconquista*: that of the partisans of the pope, who would become known as the Guelfs, and that of the emperor's party, the Ghibellines.

Of the literary works that favoured the imperial side, we must mention that of the German monk Engelbert of Admont, who wrote in 1307 and 1310, and especially the *De monarchia* of Dante (between 1310 and 1313). Among similar projects favourable to the papacy was that of Aeneas Sylvius Piccolomini, the future Pope Pius II, in 1445. Finally, in 1464 the Bohemian king George of Podebrady proposed a third way: unification by means of a league of Christian princes.

But the word 'Europe' still appeared but rarely. It was employed only by learned men, at least until the fourteenth century. We find it a dozen times in the works of Dante, who speaks of *Europae nobilissima regio* (*De monarchia*, II, 2). Note also in the same period the prophecy of Friar Jordan of Sévérac (fourteenth century) who, upon returning from India, wrote that the inhabitants had told him: 'The day will come when the Europeans shall conquer the world.' In reality, the kingdoms, which were gradually increasing their power thanks to the feudal system, did not wish to be dominated by either the pope or the emperor. The clergy and scholars who surrounded them, influenced by Roman law, drew conclusions that later would be expressed in the famous formula: 'The king is emperor in his realm.'

MODERN EUROPE, ITS CONQUESTS AND LAWS (SIXTEENTH CENTURY TO 1789)

The formation of modern states from the fifteenth century onwards can be seen concretely through the appearance of permanent armies, regular taxes and organized bureaucracies that gradually took over public affairs from the monarch's personal staff. England, France, and then reconquered Spain and Portugal were the first models, though still encumbered by feudal and seigniorial traditions.

At the very time when these states were being formed, technical innovations (gunpowder, the compass, the rudder, etc.) made possible a period of great exploration and discovery: tracing the coast of Africa at the behest of the Portuguese Prince Henry the Navigator, the 'discovery' of America by Christopher Columbus in 1492, direct access to India by way of the Cape thanks to Vasco da Gama in 1498, etc. Suddenly the world expanded in both cultural and economic terms, and Europeans became aware of their origins.

The intellectual revolution brought about by the Renaissance gave further impetus to bold thinking. The boundaries of Christendom were being stretched on all sides. The Protestant Reformation, from 1517, split western Christendom itself into several parts that were for a long time to wage war against each other.

Europe and the Turks

Yet the expansion of the Ottoman Turks might have provided an opportunity for the creation of a vast European coalition. In 1455 they took Constantinople, annihilating with one stroke the old Eastern Roman Empire. The notion of a Crusade against the Turks meant that Europe once again regarded itself as coterminous with Christendom.

This idea is found in the work of the Portuguese poet Luís Vaz de Camões, who speaks of 'poor Europe' combating the 'ferocious Ottomans'. In the same manner, Torquato Tasso considered the struggle against the Turks to be that of Europe against Asia. Erasmus also shared this view. As for Luis Vives, he wrote: 'From Gades [Cadiz] to the Ister we have a zone that stretches from sea to sea – namely, the very courageous and powerful land of Europe. There, if we were to unite with each other, we would not only equal Turkey, but would be mightier than all of Asia.' But the Crusade proved impossible. Quarrels between the contemporary states prevented it. Surrounded on three sides by the enormous kingdom of Charles V, France under Francis I went as far as to ally itself with the Turks against its enemy, even though that enemy was Catholic.

Yet it was thanks to Charles V and his successors that the rout of the Ottomans began. The victory at Lepanto (1571) was the turning-point, after which Turkey was in constant retreat until 1919.

Europe and America

America, believed to be populated by 'savages', raised an entirely different sort of problem. It was easy to conquer, but the conquerors – greedy for gold – deliberately kept the New World shrouded in mystery in order to keep the facts from their rivals. Were its inhabitants, so different from Europeans, good people? The legend of the 'noble savage' has existed since the sixteenth century, before being picked up by Jean-Jacques Rousseau. Ronsard, in his *Îles fortunées* (1553), dreamed of going there, 'far from Europe and its battles'.

America provided Europeans with food for thought and a subject for comparison. But it belonged to them as a sort of extension of Europe, as is evident from many of its place-names (New France, New Spain, New England, New Granada, Nova Scotia, New Amsterdam, New York, etc.). At the end of the eighteenth century, thanks to the American Revolution, the United States of America would become the land of liberty and 'Americanism' would flourish among European intellectuals.

Europe and Russia

Considered to be semi-barbarians, the Russians appeared on the European stage during the reign of Peter the Great (1682–1725). The maps that Montesquieu had drawn up by Robert de Vaugondy in 1756 show a 'European Russia' that stretches as far as the Volga. It would be a long time before the Urals would be spoken of as a frontier. For the moment, a great debate began, both in western Europe and in Russia, as to whether or not the Russians were Europeans in the full sense. 'Russians will never be really civilized,' wrote Rousseau (*Social Contract*, II, 8). Voltaire was unsure. The Italian Domenico Caracciolo, in his *Europe Française* (1777) argued, on the contrary, that 'Muscovy, once barbarian, today is civilized.' But civilized or not, Russia was admitted in the eighteenth century into the 'concert of Europe'.

Equilibrium and Balance in Europe

Faced with a wider world to be conquered, Europe had to endow itself with an internal organization. The dislocation of medieval Christendom and the formation of modern states gave rise to the custom of a 'European balance of power' and the rule of law. Imitating the balance of power instituted by the Italian princes in the fifteenth century, the European powers, guided by the 'reason of state', considered on the whole that their best interests lay in a certain 'equilibrium' among the principal kingdoms. Francis I of France adopted this stance spontaneously in his relations with the Emperor Charles V. Cardinal Wolsey, the English Lord Chancellor, succeeded in shifting his kingdom alternatively between alliances with Spain and with France. As William Robertson noted in his *History of the Reign of Charles V* (1769), this was 'the method for preventing any monarch from rising to a level of power that would be incompatible with general liberty'. Increasingly, treaties mentioned in their preambles that their purpose was to restore 'peace in Europe'. More and more, the great powers formed a 'concert', overseeing the affairs of the smaller states, whereas smaller states might seek to survive by placing themselves under the protection of a greater power, or occasionally by taking advantage of a need to create a 'buffer state'. But in some cases European equilibrium ended in partition, the best example of which is that of Poland.

Gradually there came into being, especially after the *De jure belli ac pacis* (1625) by Grotius, a set of rules known as the law of nations. Some wished to go even further, and elaborated proposals for a European organization that they called, after the title of Thomas More's book (1516), utopia. The most famous utopias were those of Émeric Crucé (1625), the Duc de Sully (1620-35), William Penn (1693), Jeremy Bentham (1786-89), and finally *Perpetual Peace* (*Zum ewigen Frieden*, 1795) by Immanuel Kant.

THE AGE OF NATIONALITIES (1789-1919)

At the very moment when states were interested only in the balance of power and when intellectuals were practising cosmopolitanism, there appeared - first in western Europe, then in central Europe, and finally in the Balkans - a new tendency that in the nineteenth and twentieth centuries would come to prevail the world over: national sentiment. Certainly, patriotism has always existed. People have loved the land of their ancestors and sought to expel foreign invaders. But in the second half of the eighteenth century, this raw sentiment was transformed into an elaborate concept, according to which a state was not to be defined by the vagaries of dynastic legitimacy, but rather was to coincide with a vast community, or 'nation'.

The principle of nationality was to give rise to 'nationalism' (the word first appeared in 1798 in a text by Abbé Barruel). For the pure nationalist, the nation becomes the supreme value (rather than humanity, a religion or, obviously, Europe). Thus, each nation should strive to increase its power, even if at the expense of others, who are considered to be inferior. If the principle of nationalities can easily be reconciled with the idea of a European community, it is clear that nationalism represents a disintegrative force for Europe. Indeed, it was a catalyst for war that was all the more powerful as public opinion became increasingly self-aware, and great collective passions further poisoned the conflicts started by monarchs.

Even without the will to imperialism, the principle of nationalities led to conflict, for it has a variety of different sources. With Herder, followed by Fichte, Jahn and Arndt in Germany, the idea of the nation is founded on language and popular traditions. According to the British concept of self-determination, invoked by the American colonists in 1776 to demand their independence, and the principles of the French Revolution, the nation was determined by the collective will of its inhabitants. Thus, contemporary Alsace, whose people spoke a German dialect, might be considered German according to the first principle, referred to as the Germanic or romantic one. But it was French according to the second, for its population had clearly expressed its desire to be French.

Legitimacy and Nationality Under the French Revolution

For more than a century, from 1789 to 1919, the idea of Europe found itself battling against a revolutionary change in international law. According to the principle of legitimacy, a territory belongs to its sovereign, who has the right to surrender it to another sovereign by a duly drafted and signed treaty. The adversaries of revolutionary and then imperial France, namely the traditionalists, struggled to maintain this principle. Their most brilliant theoretician, the Irish-born British Parliamentarian Edmund Burke, judged that the 'so-called rights of man' and the efforts 'to introduce them into all nations of Europe' threatened to shatter legitimacy and equilibrium. Did not France annex territories without any treaty, on the pretext that it was obeying the will of the people? It was impossible to negotiate with such a country. France must return to the 'political and economic community of all the nations of Europe'. If it did so, its power ought not to be reduced all that much, for it played an essential role in the European balance of power.

On the other hand, the revolutionaries and their partisans wanted to grant all peoples 'liberty' from tyranny. The first annexation, in 1791, was typical: Avignon and the county of Venaissin, which belonged to the pope, were joined to France following not a treaty but a plebiscite. Nevertheless, by promising to 'bring fraternity and aid to all people desirous of recovering their liberty' (decree of 19 November 1792), France embarked on a war that would soon become a war of 'revolutionary expansion'. On the pretext of bringing liberty to certain peoples, those peoples were annexed to France, the 'great nation'. Similarly, in a speech given by Danton on 31 January 1795, the ambiguous idea of 'natural frontiers' appeared. Yet, the 'enlargement of a nation arouses envy and hatred' (F. Pagès, *Histoire secrète de la Révolution française*, Vol. II). France's expansionist and revolutionary nationalism would not only help spread the principle of nationality but, by way of reaction, would also arouse ardent nationalist passions.

Napoleon and Europe

Napoleon Bonaparte led a campaign of revolutionary conquests, but in an entirely different spirit – out of ambition as a conqueror. There remains an unresolved question as to his motives: was he an imperialist pure and simple, dreaming of conquests wherever these may be? Was he a French patriot and a nationalist keen to enlarge his country, the most populous of the day? Or did he seek to unify Europe? Ultimately, his domination of the continent would prove brief. 'He is the sovereign of Europe,' wrote Metternich in 1809. In matters of theory he was far less at ease, for he addressed it only once, while on St Helena, where he reconstructed after the fact a plan that had never existed at the time of his successes. 'One of my great thoughts', he said to Count Emmanuel de Las Cases on 11 November 1816, 'was the geographic reunification or concentration of the very peoples whom revolutions and politics had dissolved, fragmented... I would have liked to bring each of these peoples together into a single body as one nation.' But this concept of Europe based on conquest clashed not only with the monarchs but also with their people.

Nationalism and the Idea of Europe in the Nineteenth Century

It was at the very moment when nationalism was increasing in range and intensity that thinkers, if not politicians, began to reflect most deeply on the idea of Europe. The general schema of this evolution begins with the rise of nationalism in liberal middle-class, republican and popular milieux. The treaties of 1815 sought to restore legitimacy. But through a series of successive stages – 1820–23, 1830–31, 1848–50, and above all from 1859 – the old order fell apart. Divided nations such as Italy and Germany were unified. The nations dominated by the Austrian Empire did not succeed in gaining their autonomy until 1918, and the same is true for Poland. But the Ottoman Empire disintegrated in Europe, and the states of Serbia, Greece, Montenegro, Romania and Bulgaria emerged one by one.

It is in these developments that we may see the seeds of the terrible wars of the twentieth century. There were a few thinkers who foresaw these and sought to avert them. They are not to be found at the side of Karl Marx and his disciples, who tried to develop a proletarian internationalism to counter the states and their nationalism, but rather among the utopian reformers such as Saint-Simon, whose project, begun in 1814, was intended to 'bring together the peoples of Europe into a single political body, while allowing them to retain their national independence', Philippe Buchez and his review entitled *L'Européen*; and Mazzini, who suggested that national and republican sentiments should be satisfied first, and then a federation of European republics could be created. The expression 'United States of Europe' first appeared in 1848, used by Henri Feugueray, a disciple of Buchez, by the Italian Cattaneo, and by Victor Hugo, who declared: 'The day will come when we shall see these two immense groups, the United States of America and the United States of Europe, join hands across the seas' (*Douze Discours*, 1850).

But the victory of Germany over France in 1871 put a halt to this development. Europe was divided into two systems of alliances whose rivalries were not eliminated by the concerted actions of the great powers. It was an armed peace. 'Anyone who speaks of Europe is wrong,' said Bismarck.

It is true, of course, that Europe mounted its last great wave of colonisation during this period. European powers conquered Africa and Southeast Asia. But instead of uniting Europeans in a common effort, the colonial venture simply transposed overseas the bitter rivalries among the states of

Europe. And the European 'balance of power', taken to its absurd conclusion, was between 1914 and 1918 to end in a bloody confrontation between the two groups of states across the impenetrable line of the trenches.

THE DRAMA OF EUROPE (1920-45)

War, Romain Rolland said in September 1914, is a 'crime against Europe'. Indeed, war, the treaties, and the post-war period were signs of its decline. The war was a sign because it was Europeans who were killing each other, ruining themselves, and in need of US intervention to settle their exhausting quarrel. The treaties, because by means of them US President Woodrow Wilson imposed a world body, the League of Nations, in place of the old 'concert of Europe' which had merely led to the war. The post-war period, because nothing was done to prevent a German nationalism bent on seeking revenge. Russia, having become Bolshevik in 1917, in the form of the Soviet Union was kept at a distance, and in any case did not conceal its desire to destroy the bourgeois regimes. A terrible economic crisis between 1929 and 1933 definitively locked Europeans into a fearful egoism, or gave rise to violent regimes, especially that of Adolf Hitler, who came to power on 30 January 1933.

Intellectuals and the Decline of Europe

The whole world was aware of this decline. It is the 'twilight of civilization,' wrote Jacques Maritain. As diverse figures as Jules Romains, Julien Benda, Henri Massis, Pierre Drieu la Rochelle and Lucien Romieu in France, Johan Huizinga in the Netherlands, Guglielmo Ferrero in Italy, Ziegler in the German-speaking lands, and Sir Arthur Salter and Hilaire Belloc in the United Kingdom described its decadence and, for the most part, considered that the only salvation lay in a European union.

But at the political level, visions were more restrained. Certainly, Aristide Briand spoke in July 1920 of a 'United States of Europe', and tried in 1929-30 to create 'a sort of federal union' of the 27 European states that were members of the League of Nations. But under no circumstances, he said, would the states lose their sovereignty. Nevertheless, no matter how modest, his project failed, primarily on account of British resistance. Similarly, Count Coudenhove-Kalergi, an Austrian diplomat, launched the idea of a 'Pan-Europe' that would gain the support of several parliamentarians. But the rise of Hitler swept away all these efforts.

Hitler's 'New Europe'

Like Napoleon, Hitler undertook to conquer Europe. Like him, he controlled it for what was a brief time from a historian's perspective, though interminable for those who suffered under his rule. But the resemblance stops there. Napoleon did not execute 6 million Jews. Hitler's Europe, the resources and population of which were exploited by the Nazi war machine, was conceived as a pyramid dominated by the great German *Reich* of 100 million inhabitants, superior to all other peoples. At his side were allies that were essentially satellites; under him, the defeated countries occupied by the Wehrmacht. Then came the protectorates or general governments of Bohemia, Poland and the eastern territories inhabited by the 'inferior race' of Slavs, which constituted the *Lebensraum* or living space. Even lower down were the Jews, subject to systematic extermination.

It was in the name of this 'new Europe' that Hitler launched his 'anti-Bolshevik crusade'. The Germans, he said, would be 'capable of providing all Europe with its leading class... The generations to come will certainly accept the unification of Europe that we are in the process of constructing.'

But this enslaved Europe, as conceived by Hitler, was defeated by the Allies and the people's resistance. It must be noted that the western resistance movements had among their most immediate preoccupations the elaboration of various proposals for a future union, of which the most remarkable was the 'Draft Declaration of the European Resistance Movements' (1944), which envisaged 'a federal union among the European peoples'.

THE IDEA OF EUROPE SINCE 1945
ALFRED GROSSER

The 'idea of Europe' might have turned into reality after 1918. Many of the combatants in the trenches had come to understand that their opponents shared the same sufferings. But French policy developed along the lines of the 'dictated peace' of Versailles. The Weimar Republic would have to live under constraint and suspicion, in the light of fears that it could not be anything other than the incarnation of 'eternal Germany'. The Franco-German 'couple' formed by Aristide Briand and Gustav Stresemann, who received the Nobel Peace Prize in 1926, embodied a different relationship, a different vision of Europe. But the crisis of 1929 and the effects of ultra-nationalism, powerfully evident in Germany from 1920 onwards, in the end allowed Adolf Hitler to take control of Germany and to impose an idea of Europe based on domination by the German people – regarded as a 'superior race' in Nazi ideology.

RECONCILIATION AS AN IMPERATIVE

If the notion of European union was not completely discredited, this was because before World War II, an entirely different concept had already found support. On 7 July 1944, a Declaration of the European resistance movements in Geneva thus called for the creation of a federal union and stated, notably: 'Only a federal union will enable the German people to join the European community without becoming a danger to other peoples.' The signatories were the members of the Danish, French, Italian, Norwegian, Dutch, Polish, Czech and Yugoslavian resistance. Among the representatives present were also Germans who were fighting Nazism.

In August 1947 the European Union of Federalists held a congress at Montreux, where they were represented chiefly by three individuals: the Italian Altiero Spinelli, who would later be responsible at the European Parliament for elaborating the draft treaty establishing the European Union, and who had just come out of Mussolini's prisons; the German Eugen Kogon, who had suffered for several years in the Buchenwald concentration camp; and the Frenchman Henri Frenay, who had been the principal leader of the 'Combat' resistance movement. Several years before the Konrad Adenauer-Alcide de Gasperi-Robert Schuman trio, they took as their starting-point the idea of a transnational co-responsibility for developing liberal democracy.

Even before the birth of their movement, the new French constitution of 1946 had tended in the same direction. The prologue (known as the Preamble and still in effect today, it has become a constant point of reference for the Constitutional Council) spoke in its first paragraph of the victory 'over the regimes that had sought to enslave and degrade humanity'. In 1919 they might have written 'over the peoples' or 'over the nations'. But the survivors of Dachau or Buchenwald knew that although these concentration camps had indeed been built by Germans, they had also been built for Germans, while on the other hand the people of France had also been less than unanimous in their resistance. The starting-point for the first Franco-German exchanges was the idea of a shared French responsibility for building democracy in the defeated country.

In this regard, the famous meetings between de Gaulle and Adenauer in Rheims cathedral, and of Kohl and Mitterand at Verdun, undoubtedly had a strong symbolic and affective power – but in a sense the symbolism was not quite right. For they appeared only to be celebrating the reconciliation that had been lacking after the first World War, whereas in fact the intention now was also to commemorate the victory over a totalitarianism that had crushed both peoples. It would have been more appropriate for the Mass and the handshake to have taken place at Dachau (given that Buchenwald was then part of East Germany).

Winston Churchill is often credited with having been the first to put forward the idea of a political union for Europe, in his famous speech in Zurich on 19 September 1946. He did indeed say there that: 'We must build a kind of United States of Europe.' But if he affirmed that 'The first step in the re-creation of the European Family must be a partnership between France and Germany', who should 'take the lead together', he also noted that the British Commonwealth was a distinct entity, as were the United States of America and the Soviet Union. Britain's absence from the European community would not change until 1973 – and even then only in a fairly uncertain fashion.

The French government's policy immediately after the war did not, in any event, follow the direction advocated by Churchill. It was concerned, rather, to control a defeated Germany as closely as possible, to maintain its disrupted unity, and to refuse to accept the creation of German organs of central administration.

THE INFLUENCE OF THE UNITED STATES

The idea of a European 'economic unit' had been put forward by the United States at the time of the Marshall Plan, launched in March 1947, essentially with a view to fostering the rebirth of free Europe's economy in face of the Soviet threat. A new directive issued by Washington in July 1947 to the general in charge of the American zone of occupation in Germany declared: 'An orderly and prosperous Europe requires the economic contributions of a stable and prosperous Germany.' In the same month, the Paris Conference brought together 16 European countries to define their needs. On 16 April 1948 the Convention for European Economic Cooperation was signed. To the 16 participants of the previous year were added the three commanders-in-chief of the American, British and French occupation forces, who signed on behalf of the western parts of Germany. As the United States had demanded in return for giving aid, the Convention gave birth to the Organisation for European Economic Cooperation (OEEC).

Parallel to an economic Europe was born a defensive Europe, a Europe with links for the purpose of defence. After the Prague coup, France, Great Britain and the three Benelux countries signed the Treaty of Brussels on 17 March 1948, directed in principle against Germany but in fact born out of fear of the Soviet Union, a fear that would lead them to ask the USA for its guarantee and support. On 4 April 1949 the North Atlantic Treaty was signed in Washington. The following year NATO, the organization resulting from that Treaty, was created. Just as in the area of economics, so too in that of defence there was an implicit idea of a Europe linked to US power.

At the political level, the notion of a specifically European union of states, launched at the Hague Congress of May 1948, met with greater difficulty. The Council of Europe, which was to give the concept more concrete shape a year later (founded on 5 May 1949), would remain simply an organization for private cooperation among the powers of the day, in accordance with the wishes of the British.

FIRST PROJECTS OF INTEGRATION: THE ECSC AND THE EDC

The actual physical effects of the new project did not really manifest themselves until 9 May 1950, with the 'Schuman plan' that proposed the creation of a European Coal and Steel Community (ECSC). Until then, France's policy toward Germany had consisted in yielding reluctantly, under pressure, to US demands. It was not without good cause that Chancellor Adenauer sent a handwritten letter to Robert Schuman in September 1962, following the highly successful visit of General de Gaulle to Germany, to express his gratitude to the man who, by virtue of the declaration made 12 years previously, had 'laid the cornerstone' for the Franco-German rapprochement and the European Community. It is appropriate that 'Europe Day' should in many countries be celebrated on 9 May, since the Schuman plan, prepared by Jean Monnet, opened up to the young Federal Republic of Germany (FDR) – created the previous year – the road to equality with the victorious countries and established for the first time, even if only in the limited fields of coal and steel, a supra-national authority.

This federation had its own specific agenda. It was not built on the concept of a nation but upon a political ethic – namely the simultaneous rejection of both the past totalitarianism of Hitler and the contemporary neighbouring one of Stalin. The German Democratic Republic (DDR), for its part, created in October 1949 by the Soviet Union, did not enjoy the legitimacy of liberty. Moreover, when in 1989–90 German reunification finally seemed possible, it was carried out in accordance with article 23 of the Bonn Constitution – that is, by the entry into the Federal Republic of Germans who until then had been deprived of their democratic freedoms.

This moral basis would continue to be reaffirmed thereafter. The German ministers of defence never invoked the words 'nation' or 'fatherland'. Thus, on 5 February 1995 when the Christian Democrat minister Volker Rühe inaugurated the first garrison of the Bundeswehr in Berlin (until 1991 the only soldiers who could be quartered there were those of the four occupying forces of the old capital in 1945), he gave it the name of Julius Leber, an assassinated socialist and member of the resistance, and declared that the re-establishment of the Bundeswehr symbolized the spirit of resistance against Nazism. And if in 1999 his successor the Social Democrat Rudolf Scharping chose 27 January to issue his memorandum announcing the intervention of the army in what had been Yugoslavia, it was because this was the anniversary of the liberation of Auschwitz, a date that since 1995 had been observed as a national day of remembrance.

Forty-five years before, it had been the very idea of German rearmament that almost killed the idea of a European unification. The Schuman plan had met with a favourable reaction – so much so that during the debate in the French National Assembly on ratification of the ECSC treaty, the Gaullist and Communist opponents of the text were obliged to justify their position against its advocates, who enjoyed the support of public opinion. But by the summer of 1951, the proposal for a European army with German participation had already aroused, in France as in Germany, significant and vigorous opposition. The French proposal for a 'European Defence Community' (EDC) was designed to conceal, under the popular mantle of 'Europe', the unpopular rearmament of Germany. On 30 August 1954, the rejection by a clear majority of French deputies of the treaty of May 1952 instituting the EDC was perceived as a destructive act by the 'Europeans' as well as by the United States, who had accepted, at France's insistence, that a European army would prevent the direct entry of the Federal Republic of Germany into NATO. On 24 October 1954 the Paris Accords granted the Federal Republic membership in NATO as the alternative solution to the EDC.

AN UNCERTAIN EUROPEAN DEFENCE

Together these two accords gave birth to the Western European Union (WEU), based on the recognition that one of the great causes for the failure of the EDC was the absence of Great Britain. Suddenly people realized the truth of the equation $5 + 2 = 6 + 1$. If to the five signatories of the 1948 treaty of Brussels (France, Great Britain, the Benelux countries) were added Italy and the Federal Republic of (West) Germany, this amounted to the same thing, in military terms, as adding Great Britain to the six members of the coal and steel community. To achieve this it was enough to remove from the 1948 text the passages aimed at a defeated Germany. The article providing for automatic military support for an ally under attack was retained – which was not the case with the North Atlantic treaty.

Later, the WEU would become the symbol, and to some extent also the reality, of a European Defence Community. The Franco-German brigade, and then the Eurocorps, would lead the way. At the time of the Treaties of Maastricht (1992) and Amsterdam (1997), 12 of the 15 members of the European Community were part of the WEU. But the position of the latter in relation to NATO, and thus in relation to the supreme US command, was never clearly established. During the bloody conflicts in the former Yugoslavia, it was difficult at times to distinguish what came under European, under NATO, or under the United Nations leadership.

In 1991, when the Gulf War broke out, the French forces intervened alongside the US and the British, while Germany limited itself to providing financial support. In 2003 Great Britain once again joined the United States against Iraq, but France and Germany refused to do so. The Maastricht Treaty rightly evokes a European defence union as a goal rather than a reality. The subject remains all the more delicate given that since the fall of the Soviet 'empire' the purpose of NATO has not yet been redefined. Poland, Hungary and the Czech Republic joined the original signatories of the alliance before acceding to the European Union, marking an even greater weakening of the EU's military role.

THE EUROPE OF THE COMMON MARKET

The failure of the EDC, followed by the birth of the WEU with British participation, may have seemed like the end of the European community. But the European project was revived in 1955 and led, in March 1957, to the signing of the Treaty of Rome creating the European Economic Community (EEC). Despite its name, the prologue to the treaty proclaimed that its purpose was political. This would be true for all subsequent treaties (Single European Act of 1987, Maastricht Treaty in 1992). But this roundabout path via economics was taken in the hope of eventually achieving a strong political integration of the six signatories. Could this hope be sustained with the fall of the Fourth Republic in France and the return of General de Gaulle to power? Had not he, and the party he created, violently opposed the Allies' policy towards Germany since 1948, as well the Schuman plan and then the Treaty of Rome?

Yet in the end, de Gaulle would rally round to the side he had for the most part denounced previously. His meeting with Chancellor Adenauer at Colombey-les-Deux-Églises in September 1958 became a symbolic act – all the more so because at the end of that year the drastic monetary reform undertaken by Antoine Pinay and Jacques Rueff restructured France's external finances, the lamentable state of which had threatened to call for a recourse to the safeguard clauses as soon as the Treaty came into force.

This change of position did not, however, eliminate some fundamental divergences. For the negotiators of the Treaty of Rome, Europe was a game of positive outcomes – that is, the totality of sacrifices agreed to by the member states was far less than the advantages that each gained from the community. For General de Gaulle, Europe would remain a coordination of sovereign states in which each sought to maximise its own advantages in relation to the others. However, he could not fail to recognize the reality of the principle that would be given forceful expression by the European Court of Justice (ECJ) in its 5 February 1963 judgment in the case of *van Gend en Loos*: 'The Community constitutes a new legal order of international law for the benefit of which the states have limited their sovereign right, albeit within limited fields.'

One of these fields was that of a common foreign trade policy. In June 1967 the Kennedy Round opened within the framework of the General Agreement on Tariffs and Trade (GATT), and ended with a European success that had been strenuously negotiated. The French government was grateful to the Belgian commissioner Jean Rey, who had spoken on behalf of the six member states and hence also of France. They agreed, a few days later, that he should become the president of the European Commission. Thirty-six years later, at the World Trade Organization (WTO) conference in Cancún, Pascal Lamy, the French EU Trade Commissioner, would negotiate the same terms on behalf of a Europe enlarged to fifteen members.

On other matters, however, General de Gaulle demonstrated a very different vision of Europe. This was manifest not only in the 'empty chair' crisis of 1964–65, when he succeeded in giving priority – intended to be a lasting one – to agriculture and to the subsidies which the European budget would grant it, but more importantly in the Franco-German treaty of 23 January 1963 and its consequences. On 14 January the President of the French Republic gave what seemed like a definitive 'no' vote to the entry of Great Britain into Europe. Was it because the country is primarily an island? That is what he said. Or because Britain rejected an integrated form of Europe – which after all he also rejected?

The contradiction was not unlike the one encountered by the treaty's adversaries in Germany, who successfully got the Bundestag to adopt a prologue to the law authorizing ratification. The latter text proclaimed the necessity of Great Britain's entry and the need for supra-nationality (sublimation of national interests in favour of communal interests), whereas London was hostile to any curtailment of national sovereignty. De Gaulle in fact hoped to use the Franco-German 'pairing' to reinforce the strength of France's voice over against the United States. As it turned out, if the Federal Republic had been faced with the choice of Paris or Washington, it would inevitably have chosen Washington. This was to be the case until 2002, when Chancellor Schröder refused all participation in the Iraq War, thus breaking with the earlier policy – at the very moment when it was being adopted by Poland, which had once enjoyed the protection of the United States against the Soviet Union.

ENLARGEMENT AND MONETARY UNION

The entry of Great Britain into the 'Common Market' occurred in 1973, after Georges Pompidou had distanced himself from the position of his predecessor, just as he had done in 1969 with regard to the devaluation of the French franc. It is true that Prime Minister Edward Heath was the first leader of the British government to have wanted to become European, while the relations between Pompidou and the German Chancellor Willy Brandt were poor. A renewed Europe, with Great Britain, Ireland and Denmark as its newest members, would deviate from the path of institutional integration, but the oil crisis of late 1973 was to lead to the discovery of a basic fact, present since 15 August 1971. On the latter date, President Nixon had decided to remove the dollar from the gold standard. From that time on there would be no ordered world monetary system. The idea thus sprang up that the European community ought to become a zone of organized monetary peace. Beginning with the Werner plan, adopted in March 1971, and ending with the adoption of the euro in 1999, via the European Monetary System of 1978 that owed much to Helmut Schmidt and Valéry Giscard d'Estaing, and by way of the Maastricht Treaty which owed much to Helmut Kohl and François Mitterand, economic union came into being through the creation of a single market on 1 January 1993, and a monetary union through the adoption of a single currency.

But the euro came into use in only 11 of the 15 member states then constituting the European Community, known since the Maastrich Treaty as the European Union. In the 1980s, the expansion of the Community from nine to twelve members was the result of a policy of political ethics. By the vagaries of fortune, Greece, Spain and Portugal emerged from a dictatorship at about the same time, in 1974–75. Economically, arguments could be made against their entry into the Community, but their request to participate in order to reinforce their nascent democracy could not be turned down.

The enlargement from 12 to 15 on 1 January 1995 was, in turn, based on sound economic and financial reasons. Finland, Sweden and Austria were democracies which needed no convincing of the idea of solidarity and political co-responsibility.

In 2004 ten new member states were admitted, in principle on account of their newly recovered liberty after the fall of the Iron Curtain (with the exception of Cyprus and Malta). But their attitude in 2003 indicated that their adherence, accepted by the Fifteen after years of complex negotiations, was no longer based on the initial political intention but more closely resembled those of the three who joined in 1995.

The same had not been true in 1990. The reunification of Germany had been carried out through the application of article 23 of the Basic Law of the Federal Republic – that is, by the entry of hitherto unfree Germans into free Germany. This meant at the same time their entry into the European Community. Article 23 was then abolished, for there was no longer anything to reunify, and replaced by another article bearing the same number and providing for the delegation of certain areas of sovereignty to the Community. In this way the treaty of unification between two states immediately imposed upon the new German states (*Länder*) a complete submission to Community norms.

A POORLY UNDERSTOOD EFFECTIVE POWER

Despite the tensions and confrontations of 2003 concerning the Convention presided over by Valéry Giscard d'Estaing and regarding a Constitution for the Europe of the Twenty-Five, these strongly restrictive norms continue to exist. It is true that the debate continues over the extension of the matters that require a qualified majority, the composition and powers of the Commission, and the application of the principle of 'subsidiarity'. It is also true that a central anomaly in the European institutional system will no doubt persist – namely, that it is the executive that makes laws. For regulations and Directives are decided by the European Council, after having been prepared by the distinct but powerful body known as Coreper, the Permanent Representatives' Committee (ambassadors). Because this fact is little known to the public, governments can in effect engage in a hypocritical game, attacking 'Brussels' on the implementation of measures that they themselves have adopted in Council, whether these are regulations directly applicable to all states or Directives that the member states must transpose into their domestic law.

It is nevertheless true that the Community's area of competence is much more vast than most citizens realize or politicians, parties and the media want to admit. In particular, the fundamental role of the European Court of Justice is often ignored, whereas national jurisdictions have all recognized its superiority. In France, the judgment of the Court of Cassation (appeal court) in the case of the *Société des cafés Jacques Vabre* of 24 May 1975, and the decision of the Council of State in the *Nicolo* case of 20 October 1989, fully admitted the superiority of the European norms. The British Parliament has on several occasions changed national legislation in order to conform to these norms. If one were to explain to a citizen of Basel or of Geneva, or to a resident of Ohio or Oklahoma, what the European Community is, one would have to say that if it were applicable in their countries it would spell the end of Swiss or American federalism. Yet Europe, which is not even confederal (neither foreign policy nor defence policy are common), has already in many regards acquired central competencies that are superior to those of federal states. Because this fact is largely ignored, however, the existence of a European citizenship, although affirmed in the treaties, is not experienced as such by its residents.

Speeches and events often allow us to forget what, three decades ago now, the French Prime Minister Jacques Chirac affirmed in his first speech to the National Assembly, on 5 June 1974: 'European policy is no longer part of our foreign policy. It is something else and is no longer separate from the fundamental aim that we develop for ourselves.'

THE ETHICAL FOUNDATION OF EUROPE

What, precisely, are the intellectual and ethical foundations of this project? What is the moral substrate of the European Union? At the Convention and thereafter, discussions on the prologue to the nascent constitution were extremely lively. One tended to forget that there is also another Europe, much larger, which has not only adopted a charter defining a political ethic but has also set up a highly effective juridical structure for implementing it. The European Court of Human Rights (ECHR) is in effect an emanation of the Council of Europe, seated at Strasbourg. It is responsible for applying the European Convention on Human Rights, signed in 1950. Since 1998 the court's judgments have been binding on member states and their jurisdictions, and national courts – including British courts – have had to bow to its decisions.

As for the ethical basis of the European Union, the most controversial point has to do with its origins, as we have seen in relation to Turkey's candidacy. Must one mention – and if so, how – Christianity, the religions, God? The conception of secularity and the role of the Churches is not the same everywhere, as is evident if we consider the differences between France and Germany. Following the example of the prologue to the Polish Constitution of 1997, however, one could take as a starting-point a set of common values held by both believers and non-believers, and argue, as did the Bishop of Clermont-Ferrand, Hippolyte Simon in a highly-regarded book, that 'It would be a grave error to try to create a holy alliance of religions against the agnostics and atheists. The distinguishing criterion here is not the belief that is proclaimed. It is rather the attitude shown toward every wounded human being that is the sign of authenticity.'

Indeed, one of the foundations of the idea of Europe has from the outset been understanding for the suffering of others. One could not ask the Germans to comprehend the full extent of the horrors of Hitler's regime without first recognizing what the bombing of Hamburg or Dresden had meant, as well as the sufferings of the 12 million people expelled from lands annexed to Poland, or from the Sudetenland. Such an understanding was created among Poles, Germans and Czechs living along the Neisse – so much so that a Euro-region known as 'Neisse-Nisa-Nysa' came into being on the two sides of the river, and in 1991 became a border fully recognized by the Federal Republic of Germany. The same sort of comprehension is still lacking between Germany and the Czech Republic concerning the Sudeten zone to the west. Still, the idea of Europe is certainly far more than simply one of economics and politics.

THE ARMENIAN GENOCIDE
CHRISTOPHE CHICLET

A vestige of the past that refuses to go away, the Armenian genocide – often considered the first genocide of the twentieth century – and its acknowledgement haunt Turkey's relations with several of its European partners. Since the 1980s, the influential Armenian presence around the world has been campaigning to have the massacres at the end of the Ottoman Empire formally described as genocide – that is, acts 'committed with intent to destroy, in whole or in part, a national, ethnic, racial or religious group as such,' according to article 2 of the 1948 Convention on the Prevention and Punishment of the Crime of Genocide.

THE DECLINE OF THE OTTOMAN EMPIRE

Under the domination of the Ottoman Empire since the fifteenth century, the Armenians nonetheless benefited, in the mid-nineteenth century, from the considerable autonomy granted to its minorities. Unfortunately, when the decline of the Empire's political and economic power began to accelerate, its position on minorities hardened. Thenceforth, the reforms applicable to the Christian minorities were ground out through pressure by the great powers. And because the Muslims of the Empire regarded these concessions as a humiliation, the minorities became the target of numerous penalties, especially in eastern Anatolia, where there was a certain degree of anarchy. To prevent massacres, the Armenians of Zeitun (modern Lamía) felt obliged to take up arms in 1859 and in 1875.

On 17 March 1863 the Sublime Porte, or Ottoman government, approved the Armenian national constitution, an instrument regulating the life of the Armenian community within the Ottoman Empire. Yet it was to be only at the Treaty of San Stefano (3 March 1878) and the Congress of Berlin (13 June – 13 July 1878) that Turkey would engage in applying reforms in its six Armenian *vilayats* (provinces). At the end of the Russo-Turkish War of 1876–78, Bulgaria recovered its independence and the Tsar occupied Batum, Kars, Ardahan and Bayazid. Article 16 of the Treaty of San Stefano also promised autonomy to the Armenians of the Ottoman Empire.

Anxious about the Russian advance towards the warm seas, Britain succeeded in having the Treaty of San Stefano reviewed at the Congress of Berlin. The Sublime Porte yielded Cyprus to Britain in exchange for its support against Russia. Article 16 was replaced by article 61, and Armenian autonomy became simply a vague promise of administrative reforms. Far from implementing these reforms, Abdul-Hamid, the 'red Sultan', decided instead to persecute the Armenians before they could gain independence as the Greeks and Bulgarians had done. During the same period, in February 1885, Russia closed its 600 Armenian schools in the Caucasus.

The community then began to organize itself politically, both within the Ottoman and Russian Empires and in the diaspora. In 1881 the secret organisations 'Defence of the Homeland' and 'Union of Patriots' were established at Erzurum and Moscow respectively. In 1885 the Armenakan Party was formed in Van and Marseilles, followed by the Social Democrat Hunchak Party in Geneva in 1887, and finally by the Armenian Revolutionary Federation (Dashnak party) in Tbilisi in 1890. The Sublime Porte could not but react, and in August 1894 the Ottoman army massacred the inhabitants of Sassun (modern Samsun). Pogroms followed throughout central Anatolia between autumn 1895 and spring 1896. More than 150,000 Armenians perished. However, at Van and Zeitun they repulsed the Turks in the course of violent skirmishes. On 26 August 1896 the Dashnak party decided to compel the great powers to enforce article 61 of the Congress of Berlin. That day, a commando of 26 militants occupied the Ottoman Bank of Constantinople, thus carrying out the first modern act of terrorism for the sake of publicity. In response the Turkish population massacred 7,000 Armenians in front of the very eyes of the western diplomats present in the capital.

The chancelleries, like the Armenians, were now given to understand that the reform policy was doomed to failure. The Young Turk Revolution and the rise of the Committee of Union and Progress in July 1908 were therefore unanimously welcomed. In its wake the constitution was re-established (23 July 1908) and Sultan Abdul-Hamid was deposed (13 April 1909). But the rejoicing would be short-lived. On 1 April 1909 close to 20,000 Armenians were massacred at Adana. The Young Turks introduced a policy of 'resolute Turkification' even as the Ottoman Empire was disintegrating, thanks in part to the Italian occupation of Tripolitania in 1911 and the Balkan Wars in 1912–13.

The Armenian National Delegation and the Armenian National Bureau then put pressure on the chancelleries, and Russia finally succeeded in getting London and Paris to modify the articles of the Congress of Berlin with respect to Ottoman Armenia. In July 1914 two inspectors-general, one Norwegian and one Dutch, were sent in to supervise reforms in the Armenian *vilayets*. World War I was then to interrupt their efforts, for the Ottoman Empire declared war against the Entente on 1 November 1914. The Armenians found themselves stuck between the two belligerent powers, the Turkish Army on the one side, the Russians on the other. The Young Turks even put pressure on the Armenians of the Caucasus to revolt against the Tsar. But this tactic provoked the opposite reaction, and soon 180,000 Armenians, of whom 8,000 were volunteers from Turkey, joined the Russian armies in order to liberate western Armenia.

On 7 April 1915 the city of Van rose up and instituted a provisional Armenian government. The reaction this provoked was as immediate as it was disproportionate. On the pretext that the Armenians were forming a 'fifth column', the Young Turk leaders Mehmed Talât, Ahmed Jemal and Ismail Enver decided to deport the entire Armenian population to the deserts of Mesopotamia. The genocide began on 24 April 1915 with the arrest and assassination of 600 Armenian dignitaries at Constantinople. The Armenian soldiers fighting in Turkish uniform were disarmed, sent to do forced labour, and then gunned down. The Armenians of eastern Anatolia were given orders to leave the country within 24 to 48 hours. Able-bodied men were shot as they left their villages, while women, children and the elderly had to walk hundreds of miles without food or medical help. Along the way they were stripped, beaten, and some had their throats slit by militiamen and by Kurdish and Turkmen tribesmen from the surrounding regions.

In August 1915 the Armenians of Cilicia and western Anatolia were deported. In the course of a little over a year, about a million (between 800,000 and 1,250,00) Armenians perished in this manner, or almost half of the Armenian population of the Ottoman Empire. The Turks are willing to acknowledge a maximum of 300,000 victims, but refuse to admit that there was a planned extermination, and thus a genocide. Instead, they blame famines, epidemics and casualties of war! But the testimonies are numerous, independent and horrifying. US and German diplomats, Swiss, US, German and Scandinavian missionaries, and German officers serving as instructors in the Ottoman army all reported the same atrocities and the same litany of the sufferings of the civilian population.

The fall of Tsar Nicholas II left the Armenians alone to face the Turks. On 3 March 1918, by the Treaty of Brest-Litovsk, Lenin ceded Batum, Kars and Ardahan to the Ottomans. Having been abandoned by the Bolsheviks, the recently-formed Legislative Assembly of Transcaucasia, or *Seim*, proclaimed the independence of Transcaucasia, which included Georgia, Armenia and Azerbaijan (22 April 1918). The Turks took advantage of these political changes and the dissolution of the Tsarist army in order to mount an offensive. Defeated by the Armenian forces led by generals Antranik and Dro at the battle of Sardarabad, they nevertheless went on to threaten the Georgians, who promptly responded by declaring their independence and requesting protection from Germany. On 28 May 1918 it was the Armenians' turn to leave the Transcaucasian Federation. But with their forces depleted and encumbered with refugees from Anatolia, the young republic was obliged to negotiate with Turkey, and its frontiers soon shrank away.

Six months later, the defeat of the Turks and of the Germans loosened the stranglehold on the republic. The Armenians reoccupied Kars and the Nakhichevan and Lorri regions. On 10 August 1920 the Treaty of Sèvres officially recognized the independence of Armenia, which became an independent state spread over about 27,000 square miles (70,000 square kilometres). Moreover, a national Armenian homeland was created in Cilicia and was made a French protectorate.

But they failed to anticipate the resurgence of Turkish nationalism under General Mustafa Kemal. On 20 October 1921 the Kemalists chased the French out of Cilicia, massacring the Armenians in the process. In the meantime, on 22 September 1920 the Kemalist forces entered the Armenian Republic with the assistance of the Azeris and the Bolsheviks. On 2 December 1920 the Armenian government was forced to renounce the Treaty of Sèvres and hand back Kars, Ardahan and the Nakhitchevan. The next day the country became a Soviet republic. The last hope of the survivors of the genocide, independent Armenia ceased to exist. From this time forward the Armenian people were faced with one of two options: to become part of the diaspora or to live under the shadow of the USSR. When the Treaty of Lausanne was signed on 24 July 1923, Armenia was not mentioned in it at all.

A DIASPORA IN SEARCH OF RECOGNITION

Out of about 7 million Armenians, almost half live in the diaspora. Survivors of the massacres of 1894 and 1915 or of the wars of 1917–21, they settled largely in the Middle East and in France. It was in the Middle East that they best preserved their cohesion, thanks to their institutions modelled on the Armenian national constitution promulgated in the Ottoman Empire in 1863 (a diocesan assembly, assisted by lay and religious executive councils). However, from 1975 onwards a great number of them left the region. As a result of the troubles in Lebanon and the Iran-Iraq war, the most significant Armenian communities in the region shrank to about half their original size. In Turkey, many left Istanbul during the latent civil war of 1976–80. Still there remained about 45,000 living in precarious conditions as a result of certain discriminatory Turkish decrees. In Anatolia, there remained a fair number of Armenians (between 2,000 and 5,000), most of them Islamicised and assimilated to the Turkish or Kurdish populations. The majority of the Armenians of the second wave of emigration went to California or to Canada. North America became the primary centre of the diaspora, with more than a million Armenians, as compared to only half a million in Europe and only about 300,000 in the Middle East.

The traditional parties continued their work in exile. The Dashnak Party was the most powerful and the least pro-Soviet. The Social Democrat Hunchak Party was completely aligned with Yerevan, as was the small Ramgavar Party, which controlled the powerful Armenian General Benevolent Union (AGBU). Together with the Armenian Communists of the diaspora they formed a common front against the Dashnaks. Nevertheless, the upheavals of 1987–88 in Soviet Armenia led some to question their support. Running parallel to these traditional parties, armed struggle and terrorism also found new groups of sympathisers. An active and virulent minority, these Armenian popular movements had their moment of glory in western Europe and in Canada between 1978 and 1983.

Yet it was undoubtedly terrorism that put the Armenian question back on the agenda. Between 1975 and 1985, nearly 160 Armenian acts of violence were officially recorded: 54 per cent of them targeted Turkish interests – the assassination of diplomats, bombs against tourist offices and airlines, commando operations in Istanbul and Ankara. Yet only 7 per cent were perpetrated on Turkish soil. Twenty-three different countries were victims, including France, target of 22 per cent of the attacks, followed by Switzerland, target of 11 per cent, and Lebanon of 10 per cent. The three main militant organizations were the New Armenian Resistance (NAR), the Commandos of Justice for the Armenian Genocide (CJAG) and the Armenian Secret Army for the Liberation of Armenia (ASALA).

The NAR mounted its first attack in Paris on 15 May 1977 and its last in Luxembourg on 28 February 1983. Its militants were mainly young European Armenians from the Maoist and pro-Third-World far left. Anti-Soviet in orientation, its members rejected blind terrorism and preferred to dissolve the group rather than be incorporated into the ASALA.

The CJAG was to become the military branch of the Dashnak Party. Originally a faction of the Middle Eastern Dashnak youth, it took up the tradition of the partisans and Armenian justice commandos of the late nineteenth and early twentieth centuries. It was the only organization that directed its actions against Turkish diplomats. Firmly established in the Lebanon and in North America, it was the target of several extremist Lebanese factions (both Arab and Armenian), as well as of the FBI. The CJAG was especially active between 1975 and 1983. The former members of this organization may have been in on the origin of the Armenian Revolutionary Army, which claimed responsibility for its last known targeted assassinations in July 1983 and June 1984.

By contrast, the ASALA was entirely different. It was founded in January 1975 by a group of young Armenians from the Lebanon working among the Palestinians. Considerably influenced by extremist Palestinians, and suffering from the Lebanese civil war, these Armenians took up the armed struggle following a theoretical model based on Stalinism. Militarily not very effective between 1975 and 1980, the

ASALA was much more concerned with political marketing. Thanks to its Palestinian allies, it succeeded in claiming responsibility for almost all 'Armenian' attacks around the world. This lent it a degree of confidence that would come to fruition among the third generation of the diaspora. Before long, young idealists from the United States, France and elsewhere joined its ranks. But the hard core, led by Hagop Hagopian, remained Lebanese.

From the summer of 1980, it took aim at the Dashnak Party members in Beirut. With frenetic paranoia, the ASALA was little by little to accuse the entire world of collusion with Turkey. When one of its militants was arrested in Switzerland or in France, the group unleashed a blind terrorist campaign against the interests of that country. Such attacks reached their peak in 1980–81. In 1982–83 the attacks were less numerous but more deadly. On 15 July 1983 the group detonated a bomb at Orly airport, Paris, leaving eight dead and 56 wounded.

Part of the organization decided to defect following this escalation. The dissension ended in a settling of scores in which ASALA militants killed each other in their camp at Bekaa (Al-Biqa, Lebanon).

Since that time the organisation has practically disappeared. It resurfaced once again, however, to assassinate important members of the Lebanese section of the Dashnak Party (March 1985 – May 1986). On 28 April 1988 Hagop Hagopian was in turn assassinated in Athens by two members of his own organization.

Terrorism by Armenians was regrettably frequent in the diaspora during the years 1975 to 1980. Such blind excesses lost Armenians credibility and thus all support from the communities. But since 1984 efforts have been increasingly directed towards gaining international recognition of the genocide committed by Turkish authorities in the early years of the twentieth century – specifically recognition by the European Parliament, which officially declared in a resolution on 18 June 1987: 'The European Parliament believes that the tragic events in 1915–17 involving the Armenians living in the territory of the Ottoman Empire constitute genocide... [and] believes that the refusal by the present Turkish Government to acknowledge the genocide [is an] insurmountable obstacle to consideration of the possibility of Turkey's accession to the Community.'

It was only much later, on 18 January 2001, that the French National Assembly unanimously passed a bill declaring that 'France publicly recognizes the Armenian genocide of 1915.' Turkey expressed its indignation. Nevertheless, a report adopted by the European Parliament on 28 February 2002 called upon Turkey to create a basis for reconciliation with Armenia. The report reiterated the EU's call to Ankara to 'take appropriate steps in accordance with its European ambitions, especially concerning the termination of the blockade against Armenia'.

Turkey's membership in the European Union will necessarily require an acknowledgment of the Armenian genocide.

THE CYPRUS QUESTION
ALI KAZANCIGIL

At the local level, the Cyprus question amounts to a conflict between the Greek community that forms the majority or about 80 per cent of the population, and the Turkish community, a minority of about 18 per cent of the population. Regionally, it constitutes one of the major subjects of dispute between Turkey and Greece. At the international level, the island situated in the middle of the eastern Mediterranean has a certain strategic value and constitutes an important launching pad and fallback position for NATO forces operating in the Middle East, thanks particularly to the British enclaves of Akrotiri and Dhekelia.

Cyprus was successively dominated by the Greeks, the Phoenicians, the Ptolemaic dynasties of Egypt, the Romans, the Lusignan family, and from 1571, the Ottomans. The Ottoman presence in Cyprus lasted exactly 307 years, until 1878, when the Sublime Porte leased the island to the British Empire. England annexed it in November 1914, when the Ottomans entered the war alongside Germany and Austria-Hungary. Cyprus was proclaimed a colony of the British crown in 1925, after Turkey had recognized its annexation by England in the Treaty of Lausanne signed in 1923.

The British presence in Cyprus was fairly well received by both communities. The Greek Cypriots hoped that the English would agree to annex the island to Greece (*enosis*), for since the Greek insurrection of 1821 against the Ottomans, Hellenism had been advancing through Cyprus. For the Turkish Cypriots, British rule was preferable to annexation to

Cyprus: a divided island

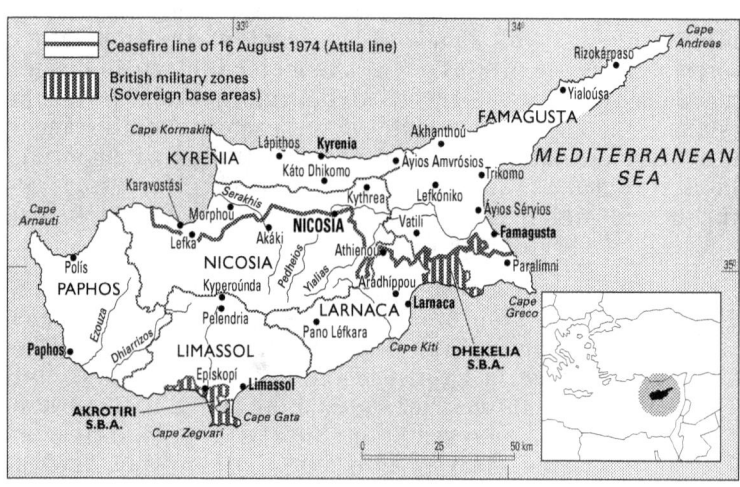

Greece. This defensive attitude on the part of the Turkish minority was to continue until the 1950s.

FROM THE ANTICOLONIAL STRUGGLE TO CIVIL WAR AND INVASION: 1945-74

From 1955 onwards, guerrilla warfare developed in Cyprus under the leadership of Georgios Grivas and the National Organization of Cypriot Fighters (EOKA), and with the support of the Church and of the right wing. The Turks responded to *enosis* by demanding the *taksim* – that is, the division of the island between Greece and Turkey. Riots against the Greek minority in Turkey occurred in Istanbul in September 1955. Thenceforth the stage was set. The conflict, initially colonial in nature, eventually became a struggle between Greek and Turkish nationalisms, with an interethnic character on the island, and an inter-state dimension within the region. Negotiations were begun that would lead to the Zurich and London Accords of February 1959, which created an independent state, having set aside both the options of *enosis* and of *taksim*. The Republic of Cyprus was proclaimed on 16 August 1960, representing a compromise between the two communities, neither of whom was willing to build a nation together. The President was Archbishop Makarios, head of the Orthodox Church of Cyprus.

The refusal of the Turks to accept a change in constitution that would eliminate their parity with the Greeks was followed, in December 1963, by terrorist acts perpetrated by Greek Cypriot members of EOKA. When in April 1967 the colonels came to power in Athens, this introduced a new factor into the Cypriot blend: the close relations between Makarios and the Athens government underwent increased strain, until finally they ruptured altogether in 1974.

On 15 July an extreme right-wing coup d'état overthrew Makarios, who was replaced by Nikos Sampson, a notorious terrorist and partisan of *enosis*. Ankara was concerned for the safety of the Turkish community, and feared that the island would be annexed to Greece. The opportunity seemed to Turkey too good to be true: Turkish forces landed at dawn on 20 July on the beaches of Kerynia, in the northern part of the island, invoking article 4 of the 1960 Treaty of Establishment, which gave them the right to intervene if the independence, territorial integrity and security of Cyprus were threatened. A ceasefire, demanded by the United Nations Security Council, was concluded on 22 July, after Turkish forces had occupied a significant part of the north of the island. On 24 July the Greek military regime that had been responsible for the coup d'état crumbled, and Constantin Karamanlis returned from exile to restore democracy to Greece. By the end of August, the Turks controlled about 38 per cent of the island's territory.

Following these operations, between 180,000 and 200,000 Greek Cypriots fled from the north to the south. In time almost all of the Greek population of the north emigrated to the south, whereas tens of thousands of Turkish Cypriots moved in the opposite direction.

IN SEARCH OF A NEGIOTATED SETTLEMENT BETWEEN PARTITION AND RECONCILIATION WITHIN EUROPE

The events of 1974 modified the power relations between the two communities. Between 1963 and 1974 Makarios had temporised, negotiating with reticence and waiting for the day when the economic blocade and pressures of all sorts would wipe out the resistance of the Turkish Cypriots. But now it was the Turkish Cypriots and Ankara who proved to be intransigent and seemed little inclined to negotiate. The first contacts between the leader of the Turkish Cypriots, Rauf Denktas, and the interim Cypriot president, Glafcos Clerides (who had replaced Nikos Sampson), took place in September 1974 in Nicosia, under the aegis of the United Nations, and concerned humanitarian questions.

In February 1975, Denktas unilaterally proclaimed the creation of a federated Turkish Cypriot state, presented as the first entity of a future federal Cypriot state. The intercommunity negotiations conducted in Vienna and New York were interrupted on several occasions on account of the intransigence of the Turkish party. The federated Turkish Cypriot state was established in February 1975 and, in the course of general elections held in June 1975, Rauf Denktaş was elected President. The Greek party continued to speak in the name of the entire island.

For more than 20 years, periods of negotiations alternated with periods of tensions, while none of the fundamental problems was really addressed: the return of Greek Cypriot refugees to the north, the percentage of the territory that would be left under Turkish Cypriot control, the retreat of foreign troops based on the island (namely the remaining 20,000 out of the 40,000 Turkish soldiers who had landed there in 1974, the other half having been repatriated between 1975 and 1978), and finally the constitutional questions, including the powers and prerogatives of the central government.

The points upon which Greek Cypriots insisted more particularly concerned freedom of movement and of residence, and the right to property, for the zone occupied by Turkey at the time held 70 per cent of the economic resources and 95 per cent of the hotel capacity on the island. As for the demilitarization of Cyprus, Denktaş – who was not prepared to accept a rapid departure of Turkish troops – spoke of the need to evacuate the two British bases, thereby embarrassing the Greek Cypriots who were enjoying considerable economic advantages from their presence, and who did not wish to bring up this question for fear it might tarnish their image as a non-aligned country.

The fundamental disagreement had to do with the notion of 'bizonality' defended by the Turks and corresponding to a fairly loose confederation, and with that of 'biregionality', proposed by the Greeks and calling for a federal type of solution, with a central government endowed with extensive powers, responsible for defence, diplomacy and finances, and leaving to the local level matters of education, culture and regional development. In addition to this constitutional question regarding the division of powers between the central government and local authorities, there remained the entire problem of the division of the territory – that is to say, the percentage of the island's territory that each of the communities would retain under its jurisdiction.

The fact that the southern part of the island had for several years been enjoying remarkable economic prosperity, and that the refugees from the north gradually found accommodation and work there, attenuated the drama of the uprooting of the population. The Turkish Cypriot leaders seemed to count on this evolution, and sought to delay the talks until a point of no return could be reached concerning the partition of the island. Meanwhile, tens of thousands of Turkish colonists were encouraged to settle in the north of the island.

The year 1983 was marked by a return of tensions and an interruption in the intercommunity negotiations. Traditionally, the Greek party had always considered that its advantage lay with an internationalization of the conflict, and was supported in this by the Soviet Union, whereas the Turkish party preferred bilateral negotiations, an approach shared by the westerners. In addition, when in autumn 1983 Greece brought the question before the General Assembly of the United Nations, the Turkish Cypriot community reacted violently, withdrawing from the negotiations then under way. In the wake of these events, Denktaş declared 'independence' on 15 November 1983, creating the 'Turkish Republic of Northern Cyprus'. This entity was recognized only by Turkey, and was unanimously condemned by the rest of the international community.

Given the decisive influence that Greece and Turkey exerted on the Greek and Turkish communities on the island, matters in Cyprus could not progress as long as Ankara and Athens did not undertake to settle their differences. Yet the fact that these two countries found themselves on the point of declaring war in March 1987, on account of their dispute concerning the Aegean Sea, came as a salutary shock to Greek and Turkish public opinion and to the two prime ministers, Papandreou and Özal.

Despite the recurring Greco-Turkish tensions, there was rarely a time between the end of the Cold War and the entry of Cyprus into Europe when conditions were as favourable to a negotiated solution as at this point. On the island, the Greek community realized that the passage of time threatened to make partition irreversible. As for the Turkish community, economically precarious and dependent on the assistance of Turkey, it was aware that it stood only to gain from a lasting peace. Finally, both Turkey and Cyprus wanted to enter the European community.

On 31 March 1998, Athens succeeded in gaining Europe's agreement to begin the process of accession in Cyprus without waiting for the conflict to be resolved. But the prospect of membership, granted in 2002, had unleashed a new force, especially among the Turkish Cypriot population. The party of Rauf Denktaş lost the elections of December 2003, and he was obliged to accept a coalition government led by the opposition leader, M. A. Talat, whose objective was to negotiate a reunification of the island on the basis of a proposal presented by the Secretary-General of the United Nations, Kofi Annan. The situation had also changed in Ankara. Although the army was highly tentative about the prospect of the disappearance of the Turkish Republic of Northern Cyprus, recognized by no one, the new AKP government was conversely pushing for an agreement among Cypriots. The European dynamic will perhaps have succeeded in ending a conflict that has raged for 40 years.

MAKARIOS III
EMMANUEL ZAKHOS-PAPAZAKHARIOU

Born in Pano Panayia, near Paphos, into a peasant family, Mikhaíl Khristódhoulos Mouskos could attend school only through the help of a monastery. After secondary school studies in Nicosia, he was ordained deacon in 1938 in the Greek Orthodox Church. Between 1938 and 1943 he studied law and theology in Athens, and served as preacher in a church in Piraeus. Ordained priest in 1946 – on which occasion he was given the liturgical name Makarios ('blessed') – he continued his studies in Boston (1946–48) with the help of the World Council of Churches. Upon his return he was named Bishop of Kition (Keti), and from that time on participated actively in the Greek Cypriot movements that were demanding the annexation of the island to Greece.

Elected Archbishop of Cyprus in 1950, he also became 'ethnarch' – that is to say, leader – of the Greek Orthodox community of the island. This title had formerly been granted by the Ottoman administration to the heads of religious communities in Europe, and involved the exercise of temporal and of administrative, economic and financial powers, as well as responsibilities for education, political representation, and even military organization. Because the Orthodox Church of Cyprus was autocephalous, Makarios had the right to hold the title of leader of the Orthodox community and could, by virtue of his position, exert great influence on the political future of the island.

The Greek population of Cyprus had, in a plebiscite held eight months earlier, expressed their wish to be united to Greece (*enosis*). Makarios became leader of this nationalist movement and travelled throughout the Western world to present and confirm the justification of the Cypriots' demand. The British government at first affected to ignore the demand, and then in 1955–56 required the governor of Cyprus, Sir John Harding, to enter into negotiations with Archbishop Makarios. In order to cut short popular protests, however, the British in 1956 deported the Archbishop to the Seychelles. Terrorist activities of the National Organisation of Cypriot Fighters (EOKA), founded in 1955 by Greek Cypriot Colonel Grivas, played a not inconsiderable role in the British decision. Nonetheless, Makarios insisted that only peaceful demonstrations be held, and disavowed EOKA.

The deportation of the Cypriot leader was carried out in somewhat chaotic fashion – Makarios' plane was diverted to the Seychelles when he was actually flying to London to discuss the conditions of self-determination for Cyprus. Terrorist activity increased on the island as a result. The Turkish Muslim community of Cyprus consequently took up arms against EOKA and demanded that the island be annexed to Turkey. The last thing London and Washington wanted was to see a conflict between two members of NATO, and so negotiations between Turkey and Greece were opened in Athens. Set at liberty again, Makarios took part in the talks. Arguing for a peaceful solution, he gained independence for the island, and in December 1959 became head of the new state.

Very soon he had to confront the partisans of annexation to Greece – General Grivas and EOKA as well as a deputation from the Orthodox Church of Cyprus, led by Bishop Kyprianos. Makarios neutralized Grivas by giving him command of the armed forces, and worked towards rapprochement between the Orthodox and Muslim communities. In 1964, taking advantage of the occasion of the rise to power in Athens of centrist forces led by Georgios Papandreou, and faced with bloody confrontations between the two island communities, he demanded that the accords defining the status of Cyprus be revised, and sought to introduce a clause that would bring about *enosis*. But the fall of Papandreou, and Grivas' close ties with the colonels that thereafter formed a ruling junta in Greece, pushed Makarios to insist on complete independence for the island under a system that would respect the existence of both communities.

Having won an overwhelming mandate at the elections of 1968, and supported by the centrist labour party and the Communist left (Progressive Party of the Working People, or AKEL), Makarios broke with Grivas' nationalists and purged the Church of nationalist prelates. He escaped several attempts on his life. The death of Grivas in January 1974 presented him with a further means of visible independence from the activities of the Greek nationalists. Makarios demanded that Greece recall the Greek officers who had served as the core of the Cyprus National Guard. But even before Athens could react to his demand, the Greek officers based in Cyprus incited the national guard to revolt. Makarios, whose death had already been announced – wrongly – was formally deposed on 15 July 1974 and forced to flee to London.

Greek and Turkish troops intervened. In August, Glafcos Clerides, head of the Cyprus government, had to leave Nicosia for Limassol. In December, Makarios returned to Nicosia, where he received a triumphal welcome and resumed the leadership of the government, continuing in this capacity until his death on 3 August 1977.

BIBLIOGRAPHY

AMIRAUX, V. (2001) *Acteurs de l'islam entre Allemagne et Turquie: parcours militants et experiences religieuses.* Paris: L'Harmattan.

BARKEY, H. J. and G. E. FULLER (1998) *Turkey's Kurdish Question.* Lanham, NY: Rowman & Littlefield.

BASRI ELMAS, H. (1998) *Turquie, Europe, une relation ambiguë.* Paris: Syllepse, 1998; 'L'intervention du facteur «immigration» dans les relations turco-européennes', in *Revue européenne des migrations internationales,* 4: 77–101.

BAZIN, M., S. KANÇAL, R. PEREZ and J. THOBIE (1998) *La Turquie entre trois mondes.* Varia Turcica, XXXII. Paris: L'Harmattan.

BERTRAND, G. and I. RIGONI (2000) 'Turcs, Kurdes et Chypriotes devant la cour européenne des droits de l'homme: une contestation judiciaire de questions politiques', in *Études internationales,* vol. 51, no. 3: 413–41.

BILLION, D. (1997) *La Politique extérieure de la Turquie.* Paris: L'Harmattan.

BLANC, P. (2000) *La Déchirure chypriote.* Paris: L'Harmattan.

BOZARSLAN, H. (1997) *La Question kurde. États et minorités au Moyen-Orient.* Paris: Presses de Sciences-Po.

BOZARSLAN, H. (2000) 'Kurdes: autonomie en Irak, radicalisation en Turquie', in *Universalia 2000,* pp.206–9. Paris: Encyclopedia Universalis.

BRUINESSEN, M. van (2000) 'Transnational aspects of the Kurdish question', RSCAS working paper, Florence: European University Institute.

BRUINESSEN, M. van (2001) *Kurdish Ethno-Nationalism.* Istanbul: ISIS.

BRUINESSEN, M. van (2002) *Mullas, Sufis and Heretics*. Istanbul: ISIS.

ÇAKIR, R. (1995) 'La Ville, piège ou tremplin pour les islamistes turcs?' in *Cahiers d'études sur la Méditerranée orientale et le monde turco-iranien* 19: 183-96.

CIZRE, U. (2003) 'Demythologizing the national security concept: the case of Turkey', in *Middle East Journal*, vol. 57, no. 2 (spring).

Confluences Méditerranée: les Kurdes, special number 34 (2000).

DANIEL, G. (2000) *Atatürk, une certaine idée de la Turquie*. Paris: L'Harmattan.

DEDEYAN, G. (1982/1986) *Histoire des Arméniens*. Toulouse: Privat.

DELI, F. (2000) 'Les Flux migratoires de populations originaires de Mardin vers Istanbul', in I. Rigoni, ed. *Turquie: les milles visages*. Paris: Syllepse.

DORRONSORO, G., E. MASSICARD and J.-F. PÉROUSE (2003) 'Turquie: changement de gouvernement ou changement de regime?', in *Critique internationale*, 18 (January): 8-15.

DUMONT, P. (1997) *Mustafa Kemal invente la Turquie moderne: 1919-1924, la mémoire du siècle*. Brussels: Ed. Complexe.

FULLER, G. E. and I. O. LESSER (1993) *Turkey's New Geopolitics: From the Balkans to China*. Boulder, CO: Westview Press.

GOKALP, A. (1998) 'L'Islam des Turcs', in *Hommes et migrations*, no.1212 (March-April): 35-52.

GÖLE, N. (1993) *Musulmanes et modernes. Voile et civilisation en Turquie*. Paris: La Découverte.

GROC, G. ed. (1999) 'Formes nouvelles de l'Islam en Turquie', in *Les Annales de l'autre islam*, no. 6.

GROSSER, A. (1978) *Les Occidentaux. Les pays d'Europe et les États-Unis depuis la guerre*. Paris: Fayard.

GÜRBEY, G. and F. IBRAHIM, eds (2000) *The Kurdish Conflict in Turkey. Obstacles and Chances for Peace and Democracy*. New York: St Martin's Press.

'Laïcités en France et en Turquie', in *Cahiers d'études sur la Méditerranée orientale et le monde turco-iranien*, no. 19 (1995).

LEQUESNE, C. and A. SMITH, eds (1997) 'Interpréter l'Europe', in *Cultures et conflits*, no. 28.

'L'Individu en Turquie et en Iran', in *Cahiers d'études sur la Méditerranée orientale et le monde turco-iranien*, no. 26 (1998).

MANTRAN, R. (1990) *Histoire de l'Empire ottoman*. Paris: Fayard.

MANTRAN, R. (1993) *Histoire de la Turquie*. Paris: P.U.F.

MANTRAN, R. (1994) *Istanbul au siècle de Soliman le Magnifique*. Paris: Hachette.

MARDIN, S. (1997) 'La Religion dans la Turquie moderne', in *Revue internationale des sciences sociales*, no. 29.

MARDIN, S. (1989) *Religion and Social Change in Modern Turkey. The Case of Bediüzzaman Saïd Nursi*. New York: University of New York Press.

MARDIN, S. (2000) *The Genesis of Young Ottoman Thought*. Syracuse, NY: Syracuse University Press.

MASSICARD, É. (2003) *Les Élections du 3 novembre 2002: une recomposition de la vie politique torque?* Dossier de l'IFEA (July).

NAUCK, B. (1994) 'Transformations démographiques de la population torque immigrée en Allemagne', in N. Bensalah, ed. *Familles turques et maghrébines aujourd'hui. Évolution dans les espaces d'origine et d'immigration*. Louvain-la-Neuve: Academia, pp.55-73.

ÖKTEM, E. (1999) 'La Cour constitutionnelle turque définit le nationalisme, principe de la république', in *Revue de droit public et de la science politique en France et à l'étranger*, no. 4: 1159-1200.

PICARD, É. ed. (1991) *La Question kurde*. Brussels. Ed. Complexe.

RIGONI, I. ed. (2000) *Turquie, les mille visages*. Paris : Syllepse.

RUBIN, B. and M. HEPER, eds (2002) *Political Parties in Turkey*. London: Frank Cass.

SAKTANBER, A. (2002) *Living Islam: Women, Religion and the Politicization of Culture in Turkey*. London: Tauris.

TAPIA, S. de (1996) *L'Impact régional en Turquie des investissements industriels des travailleurs émigrés*. Paris: L'Harmattan.

TAPPER, R. ed. (1991) *Islam in Modern Turkey*. London: Tauris.

VANER, S. (1995) 'Turquie: la nouvelle donne', in *Problèmes politiques et sociaux*, no. 757, Paris: La Documentation française.

WANNER, P. (2002) 'Migration Trends in Europe', in *European Population Papers*, no. 7.

WHITE, J. B. (2002) *Islamist Mobilization in Turkey: A Study in Vernacular Politics*. Seattle: University of Washington Press.

YERASIMOS, S., G. SEUFERT and K. VORHOFF, eds (2000) *Civil Society in the Grip of Nationalism*. Istanbul: Orient Institute and French Institute of Anatolian Studies (IFEA).

ZÜCHER, E. J. (1993) *Turkey: A Modern Story*. London: Tauris.

ADDITIONAL INTERNET RESOURCES

To consult additional Internet resources provided by the *Encyclopaedia Universalis*, visit **www.universalis.fr** where the following sections are relevant:

1 **Turkey – a world apart, or Europe's new frontier?**
   - TURKEY: CURRENT EVENTS, 1990–2003.
   - 2003 REGULAR REPORT ON TURKEY'S PROGRESS TOWARDS ACCESSION, European Commission (December 2003).

2 **Turkey – a democracy under control?**
   - PORTRAIT OF ALPARSLAN TÜRKES, by Chritsophe Chiclet.
   - PORTRAIT OF SÜLEYMAN DEMIREL, by Ali Kazancigil.
   - PORTRAIT OF BÜLENT ECEVIT, by Ali Kazancigil.
   - PORTRAIT OF TURGUT ÖZGAL, by Christophe Chiclet.

4 **Islam in Turkey: a 'secular Muslim' state**
   - SUNNISM, by Roger Arnaldez.
   - SHIISM, by Henri Corbin and Yann Richard.
   - ISLAM AND THE STATE, by Olivier Roy.
   - THE BEKTASHIYYA, by Vincent Monteil.
   - THE NAQSHABANDIYYA, by Vincent Monteil.

5 **Turkey and the European Union: from migration to integration?**
   - THE TURKS, by Robert Mantran.
   - TURKISH POPULATIONS, by Emmanuel Zakhos-Papazakhariou.
   - WHAT KIND OF A MIGRATION POLICY SHOULD EUROPE ADOPT? by Catherine Wihtol de Wenden.

6 **Can the Kurdish question be resolved within Europe?**
   - MINORITY RIGHTS, by Yves Plasseraud.
   - THE KURDS, by Thomas Bois, Hamit Bozarslan, Christiane More, and Éric Rouleau.
   - PORTRAIT OF MUSTAFA BARZANI, by Christian Bromberger.

7 The Ottoman Empire
- THE SELJUKIDS, by Robert Mantran.
- THE BYZANTINE EMPIRE, by José Grosdidier de Matons, Claire Jolivet-Lévy, and Jean-Pierre Sodini.
- PORTRAIT OF SÜLEYMAN THE MAGNIFICENT, by Robert Mantran.

8 Mustafa Kemal Atatürk
- PORTRAIT OF CELÂL BAYAR, by Robert Mantran.
- PORTRAIT OF ISMET INÖNÜ, by Jean-Charles Blanc.

10 The idea of Europe since 1945
- CHRONOLOGY OF THE CONSTRUCTION OF EUROPE.
- THE EUROPEAN CONVENTION ON HUMAN RIGHTS, by Jacqueline Demaldent.
- THE CHARTER OF FUNDAMENTAL RIGHTS OF THE EUROPEAN UNION, by Didier Maus.

11 The Armenian Genocide
- ARMENIA, by Jean-Pierre Alem, Christophe Chiclet, Sirapie Der Nersessian, Kegham Fenerdjian, Hervé Legrand, and Marguerite Leuwers-Haladjian.

12 The Cyprus question
- CYPRUS, CURRENT EVENTS 1990–2003.

13 Makarios III
- PORTRAIT OF GEORGES GRIVAS, by Nikos Athanassiou and Liliane Princet.

GLOSSARY

ALEVIS: Members of a heterodox and syncretistic religious community that constitutes a significant minority in Turkey, recruiting among both Turks and Kurds. Probably the result of an encounter between the shamanism of nomadic Turcomans and Shiite Islam, Alevism remains quite mysterious in nature: it follows an esoteric interpretation of Islam and has several distinctive practices of uncertain origin. Strongly involved in politics, Alevis have sometimes been subject to violence by fundamentalist Sunnis, who consider them to be heretics.

ATLANTICIST: Describing a policy of military cooperation between European and North American powers, notably – but no longer specifically – in the form of the North Atlantic Treaty Organization (NATO).

CALIPHATE: The dignity, power and authority of the head of the Muslim community, the successor of the Prophet on earth. Initially the Caliph ('successor') combined both religious and political functions, but soon lost his political authority in favour of the Sultan, who was the *de facto* ruler. In 1517 the Ottoman Sultan was proclaimed Caliph, thus bringing the two functions back together again, but this time to the advantage of the political authority. In 1924 Atatürk abolished the caliphate and, despite a few efforts, this function has never been re-established.

COPENHAGEN CRITERIA: The European Council meeting in Copenhagen (June 1995) defined the criteria that candidate countries for membership in the European Union, including

Turkey, must fulfil before their accession (see Table 0, page 00). These criteria concern:

- the presence of stable institutions guaranteeing democracy, the primacy of the rule of law, human rights, respect and protection for minorities (political criterion);
- the existence of a viable market economy as well as the ability to withstand competitive pressure and market forces within the European Union (economic criterion);
- the capacity of the candidate country to take on the obligations following from accession, namely to subscribe to the political, economic and monetary objectives of the Union (criterion of the acceptance of the Community *acquis*, or terms and conditions).

ISLAMISM: Political doctrine based upon the political model of the early years of Islam; it turns religion into a political ideology capable of assimilating modernity. Islamism insists on the need to set up an Islamic state, with its own institutions and laws founded on the *sharia* (Islamic law). In Turkey, Islamism has found concrete expression in various political parties such as the Refah, now dissolved, but is at present in decline, to the point that the successor party to the Refah (AKP) refutes this term.

JACOBIN: Modern term derived through French to describe radical extremism aimed at total political democracy. When opposed, adherents may well engage in terrorist activities.

KEMALISM: Set of principles centred on imitating the West, elevated practically into an ideology, which were at the basis of the reforms undertaken by Atatürk. It is often summed up as six principles: republicanism (against the caliphate and the sultanate), secularity, progressivism (universal education and promotion of women), populism (rejection of social hierarchies inherited from the past, the myth of a homogeneous, unified Turkish people), statism (the aim to achieve a strong state, of which the army constitutes the principal pillar, and a state-controlled economy), and nationalism.

OTTOMANISM: The sense of nostalgia for the Ottoman Empire, the religious legitimacy of which was combined with a broad ethnic diversity. The non-Muslim groups were organised according into *millets* (ethno-religious communities) free to practise their religion, while non-Turkish Muslims were able to build a career by virtue of their loyalty to the person of the Sultan. But this model has not survived the rise of nationalism.

PAN-TURKISM: The ideology developed at the end of the nineteenth century according to which all Turkish-speaking populations in the world share a common ethnic origin and have a vocation to be gathered into one common political unit. Pan-Turkism is in contradistinction with Kemalism, for it considers the Turkish republic a merely temporary means to an end, whereas Kemalism considers it an end in itself. It also opposes the principles of the caliphate, which considers religion (Islam) and not race to be the basis for an empire led by the Turks. Pan-Turkism may be secular or be marked by pan-Islamism.

RELIGIOUS FRATERNITY: (*tarikat*) Disciples of a *Pir* (patron) or a *Sheikh* (master) who meet to practise elaborate forms of devotion, mainly *zikr* or *dhikr* (a sort of litany repeated with the intention of glorifying God). The great founding masters (such as Bahauddin Nakshband for the Nakshbandis) delegated their power to representatives who in turn could create new fraternities. The development of these fraternities in the most varied settings may be explained by complex and flexible chains of transmission (with schisms and fusions), by the great mobility of *pirs* and their disciples, by the search for more mystical forms of spirituality, and finally by the wide spectrum of different sensibilities expressed by each fraternity. In Turkey these fraternities play an indirect political role as agents of mobilisation, especially for elections.

STATISM: A policy or the situation in which a nation's economic controls and planning are concentrated in the hands of state apparatus.

SUNNISM: The dominant school within worldwide Islam. It defined itself in distinction to Shiism, which affirmed that the Caliph is a 'successor' to the Prophet, whereas the Sunnis claim he is chosen by the community. Sunnis never developed a hierarchical or organised clergy: the sect is divided into different schools of law, which are not antagonistic to each other but which govern the laws in the territory where they are in the majority. Thus the Ottoman Empire and present-day Turkey are Hanafite (named after the founder of that school, Abu Hanifah), while the Kurds are Shafites (named after Imam Shafei). The differences between schools often have to do with points of detail that may be little known to the majority of believers themselves.

TANZIMAT: ('reforms') Name for the period of reform 1839–1876 begun by Sultan Abdu Mecit in order to rationalize the administrative and political system (citizenship, conscription, fiscal system, and finally the promulgation of a Constitution, stillborn in 1876). The reforms were cancelled in 1876 by Sultan Abdul Hamit II.

YOUNG TURKS: Nationalist and protest movement, led in part by young officers, that appeared at the very beginning of the twentieth century and which tried to reform the state and return to the Constitution of 1876 enacted by the liberals in order to structure the Ottoman Empire. In 1908 the Young Turks came to power peacefully and deposed the Sultan, but their reforming plans were thwarted by the Empire's defeats: the Balkan wars, then the First World War. In 1919 they yielded power to one of their own: Mustafa Kemal.

INDEX

References to maps, have the suffix m. References to the glossary have the suffix g.

Abdul-Hamid II 113-4, 120, 164-5
Adalet Partisi 34, 65
Adenauer 132, 150, 152, 155
Adrianople 108, 112, 115
  Treaty of (1713) 15, 97, 99, 104, 107
Aegean Sea 3, 14-16, 24, 97, 101-102, 133, 178
Afghanistan 22, 62, 129
Africa 67, 101-3, 109, 111, 113, 115, 133, 139
Akkerman, Treaty of 111
AKP (Justice and Development Party) xii, 19, 21, 24, 35, 52, 65, 68, 179
Alawites 57
Albania 57, 102
Alevis 57, 78, 191g
Aliev, Heydar 21
al-Qaeda 4, 21
America (discovery of) 139-140
  see also United States (US)
Amsterdam, Treaty of 72, 154
Anatolia 1, 6, 15, 58, 62, 121-6, 163-8
  and Ottoman Empire 93-9, 102, 104, 112, 116-117

Andronicus III 96
Ankara 2, 6, 14, 17, 22, 63, 79, 81, 86-9, 99, 117, 122, 125, 129, 168
  Treaty of 72, 129
Armenia 18-22, 55, 81-2, 88, 114, 123-5, 163-71
Armenian Revolutionary Party (Dashnak) 164, 168-170
Armenian Secret Army for the Liberation of Armenia (ASALA) 169-170
Atatürk, Mustafa Kemal ix, 1, 20, 40, 54, 82, 93, 116-30, 167
Auschwitz 153
Austria 13, 69, 108-10, 113-14, 158
Azerbaijan 21-2, 102, 107, 166

Balkan wars 115, 165, 194
Balkans, The 11-12, 20, 57, 93, 97-8, 101, 104, 113, 116, 141
Barzani, Mustafa 84
Bayezid I 98-9
Bayezid II 102
Bektashis 57
Belgium 69, 114
  see also Brussels

Bismarck 113
Black Sea 80m, 92m, 93, 100, 102, 105, 109, 133
  Treaty 22
Bosnia 21, 62, 102, 113
Bosporus 14, 53, 112
Brussels 17, 67, 76, 87–89
  Treaty of 152
  see also Belgium
Bucharest, Treaty of 110
Buchenwald 150
Bulgaria 57, 110, 113, 116, 120, 129, 145, 164
Burke, Edmund 143
Byzantium 11, 15, 93–7, 100, 135–6

caliphate ix, 2, 12–13, 53–4, 82–3, 103, 117, 124–5, 191–3g
Cantacuzenus, John 96
Caucasus 11–12, 21–2, 120, 164
cemaat 59–60
Charlemagne 131, 136, 137
Charles V 140
Chechnya 20–21
Chirac, Jacques 160
Christianity 13, 33, 105
  'Christian Club' 24, 53, 63, 78
  and Europe 65, 103, 134–41, 153, 161
  and Islam 54–5, 82–3, 94, 97, 101–2, 111–13, 131, 136, 163
Churchill, Winston 151
Cilicia 102, 122, 166
civil war 5, 21, 79, 84
Clerides, Glafcos 183
Cold War 132, 179
Commandos of Justice for the Armenian Genocide (CJAG) 169

Congress for Freedom and Democracy in Kurdistan (KADEK) 81, 87
Congress of Berlin 113, 164–5
Constantinople 11, 15, 54, 93, 98, 101–7, 110, 113–16, 165
  see also Istanbul
constitution, Turkish ix, 27–8, 31–2, 37, 50, 54, 65, 114, 126
Copenhagen criteria x, xii, 23–4, 37, 68, 86, 191–2g
coups 31, 65, 74, 152, 175–6
  1960 x, 27, 31
  1980 x, 27, 34, 38, 56, 70
  1983 17
Crete 108, 111, 113, 116
Crimean War 112
Cyprus x, 3, 5, 14–16, 19, 24, 31, 79, 88–9, 107, 113, 158, 164, 173–83, 174m

Dachau 150
Damascus 15, 79, 120
Dardanelles, The 14, 96–7, 116
Denktaş, Rauf 176–7, 179
de Gaulle, Charles 150, 155–7
democracy 3, 5, 23, 25, 32–3, 68, 89, 150, 153, 158
Denmark 6, 69, 149
Dervis, Kemal 52
Directorate of Religious Affairs (DIB) 54–5
Diyenet 55–6, 59
DSP 35

'Eastern Question' 109–111
Ecevit, Bülent 2, 19, 25, 36
Economic Cooperation Organisation 22–3
Economy, Turkish xi, 5, 18, 30, 37–52, 61, 70, 128, 192g

INDEX 197

Egypt 102-4, 107, 110-113
Elchibey, Abulfaz 21
Elevis 191g
England *see* Great Britain
enosis 16, 175, 182
Erbakan, Necmettin 21, 33, 61, 64, 65
Erdogan, Recep Tayyip xii, 16, 29, 31, 33, 36, 68
Erzurum 121-2, 164
Estaine, Giscard d' 15, 24, 68, 158-9
European Coal and Steel Community (ECSC) 152-3
European Common Agricultural Policy (CAP) 43
European Council x, 159
European Defence Community (EDC) 152-5
European Economic Community (EEC) 70, 155
European Free Trade Association (EFTA) 43
European Union (EU) 1-3, 5, 12, 24, 31, 37-9, 43-6, 52, 65, 67, 69, 70-72, 77-81, 86-7, 150, 155, 160-61, 171
Evran, Kenan 34

Far East 106, 109
fatwas 7
Felicity Party 64
Finland 88, 158
Foreign Direct Investment (FDI) 51
foreign policy 75, 115
  Turkish 12, 19, 79, 128
France 3, 14, 22, 67-72, 76, 82, 98, 104-106, 109-16, 120-23, 129, 139-145, 149-57, 161, 165-6
Frenay, Henri 150

Gallipoli 96, 120
Gastarbeiter (guest workers) 71-3
Gaul 131, 135-7
  see also France
General Agreement on Tariffs and Trade (GATT) 156
Georgia 21-2, 107, 166
geography, Turkish xiv(m), 4, 11, 12, 77, 80m, 96, 133
Germany 3, 14, 33, 45-6, 67-77, 98, 113-16, 120, 137, 142-9, 150-61, 166
Ghazi 95
Grand National Assembly (GNA) 122-8
Great Britain 6, 14-15, 25, 69, 82, 98, 106,109-16, 120, 129, 139, 151-7, 164-5, 173
Greece 3-4, 13-18, 24, 55, 82, 96, 101, 111-17, 123-5, 129, 131-4, 145, 158, 168, 173-5, 182-3
Greek Cypriots 175-8, 181
Grivos, Georgios 175, 182-3
Gulf War (1991) 154

Hagia Sophia 63, 107
Hanafite Sunnism 56-7
Hitler, Adolf 132, 146-7, 149, 153, 161
Hizbullah 62, 85
Holland 67, 69, 106, 109, 149, 165
homogeneity 11, 13, 29, 55, 73, 192
human rights x, xiii, 3, 17, 23, 25, 68, 77, 86, 88, 132, 160
Hungary 98-9, 102, 107, 108, 155
Hussein, Saddam 79

IMF (International Monetary Fund) 49, 52
immigration 6, 24, 71-4, 77-8
India 18, 109, 114, 138-9
inflation 46-8, 52
Inönü, Ismet 120, 125
integration (Turks into Germany) 71-5
Iran 4, 14, 17, 23-4, 57, 70, 81, 114, 129, 168
Iraq 103-4, 125, 129
  geography xiv(m) 17, 24, 80m
  and Iran 4, 98, 168
  Kurds 6, 17, 70, 79, 81-2, 84, 87, 89
  US invasion (2003) 4, 22-3, 25, 36, 52, 87, 155, 157
ISAF 22-3
Islam
  and Ataturk 1, 119, 129
  and Christianity Islam 54-5, 82-3, 94, 97, 101-2, 111-13, 131, 136, 163
  and Europe 3, 12, 24-5, 182
  and Kemalism 18-21, 54
  and Ottoman Empire 95-6, 104, 129, 163, 168
  and secular state 6, 53-63
Islamism 2, 17-20, 27, 32, 75-6, 192g
  political parties xi, 21, 25, 29, 63, 65
Islamist Refah Party (RP) xi, xii, 19, 21, 29, 61, 63-4, 128
Ismaïl, Shah 102
Israel 4, 14, 21, 22-3, 55
Istanbul 4, 6, 11, 20-21, 55, 63, 69, 101, 107, 119-25, 168, 175
  see also Constantinople

Italy 82, 98, 113-16, 120, 123, 129, 131-3, 136-7, 145, 149
Izmir 15, 109

Jacobin 5, 12, 192g
Jews xii, 13, 23, 55, 147
Justice and Development Party (AKP) xii, 19, 21, 24, 35, 52, 65, 68, 179

Karlowitz, Treaty of 108
Kemal, Mustafa ix, 1, 20, 40, 54, 82, 93, 116-30, 167
Kemalism x, 5-6, 12-13, 17-20, 23-5, 30, 33, 55-56, 65, 75, 82-4, 88, 130, 167, 192g
Keussem 108
Khan, Genghis 94, 98
Kilinc, Tuncer 37
Kirkuk 79, 89
Kizilbash 57
Kogon, Eugen 150
Kohl 150, 158
Kongra Gel (People's Congress) 81
Korea 14-15
Kuchuk-Kainarji, Treaty of 109
'Kurdish question' 4-6, 17-19, 24-5, 63, 79, 80m, 81-9, 116
Kurdistan 5, 17, 80m, 81-4, 87, 89, 92m, 103
Kurds 166-8
  and Islam 56-7, 62, 75, 168
  and language 13, 67
  as a minority 12, 29, 33, 70
  and nationalism 32, 36, 76-7
Kutahya, Treaty of 112

language
  Kurdish 13, 18, 24, 67, 76-7, 86-7

spoken Turkish 13, 57, 100
written Turkish 1, 20, 54, 126–7
Lausanne, Treaty of (1923) ix, 13–16, 33, 82, 117, 167, 173
League of Nations 129, 146–7
Lebanon 84, 112, 169
Libya 21

Maastricht Treaty 155, 158
Macedonia 113, 116
Mahmud II 110
Makarios III 16, 181–3
Makarios, Archbishop 175–6, 181–3
Marmara 42, 96 (sea of)
Marx, Karl 145
Marxism 6, 33, 145
Mecca 55, 136
media 76–7, 86, 122
Mehmed I 99
Mehmed II 99–102
Mehmed VI 121, 124
Mehmed Ali (Muhammad Ali) 111–112
Mehmed Keuprulu 108
MHP (right-wing nationalists) 18
Middle East 2, 11–12, 19, 24, 69, 81, 84, 87, 167, 173
migrants (from Turkey) 3, 6, 67–74, 77–8
Milli Görüş (national vision) 61
Mitterand 150, 158
Moldavia 107
Montreux convention (1936) 14, 129, 150
Murad I 97–8
Murad II 99
Murad III 104, 107
Murad IV 108
Mustafa IV 110

Napoleon 110, 144, 147
Naqshabandiyya 57, 59
National Intelligence Council (MIT) 31
National Planning Office (DBT) 32
National Order Party (NMP) 61
National Organisation of Cypriot fighters (EOKA) 182
National Salvation Party (MSP) 61, 63
National Security Council (MGK) 27, 31–2, 34, 37, 194
nationalism 2, 13, 20, 24, 33, 142, 144
NATO (North Atlantic Treaty Organisation) ix, 2, 11, 14–15, 19, 22–24, 30, 152–55, 173, 182
New Armenian Resistance (NAR) 169
Nicolas I, Tsar 111
Nicolas II, Tsar 166–7
Nicosia 183
Nixon, Richard 158
Norway 69, 149, 165

Öcalan, Abdullah xi, 17, 81, 85, 87
oil 22, 114, 157
Orkhan 95–7
OSCE 22, 23
Osman 95–7
Osman II 107
Otto III 137
Ottoman Bank 128, 165
Ottoman Empire ix, 11–19, 81–2, 92m, 93–103, 100–101, 106–117, 145, 163–8
  and religion 53, 63, 125, 129, 173, 181
  and World War I 120, 123, 140

Ottomanism 20, 55, 192g
Ouchy, Treaty of 115
Özal, Turgut x, 5, 17-18, 20, 34, 38, 178

Pakistan 18, 23
Palestine 4, 103, 116, 120-21, 169
pan-Islamism 21, 114
pan-Turkism 12, 13, 19-20, 115, 193g
Papandreou 178, 182
Paris, Treaty of 112
Parliament (Turkish) 28, 33-6, 62
Pasha, Ismet 123
Passarowitz, Treaty of 109
Peloponnese 102
PKK (Kurdistan Workers' Party) xi, 5-6, 17, 29-30, 77, 79, 81, 84-5, 87
Poitiers, Battle of 131, 136
Poland 25, 108, 141, 147, 149, 155, 157, 161
Pope 137-8, 143
 Pius II 138
 Gregory VII 137
Portugal 3, 4, 139, 158
Potsdam Conference 14

Qur'an 58-9, 64, 127

Refah (Welfare) Party xi, xii, 19, 21, 29, 61, 63-4, 128
republic ix, 6, 55-56, 82, 88-9, 117, 124, 126
Republican People's Party (CHP or PHP or RPP) 19, 34, 35, 125-7
Right Way Party (DYP) 63
Romania 100, 113, 129, 134, 145
Rome, Treaty of x, 72, 155-6

Russia 44, 108-113, 116-7 140-41, 164-5

Saddam Hussein 79
Salonica 115, 119-20
San Stefano, Treaty of 164
Sandjak of Alexandretta 15, 129
Saudi Arabia 69
Schengen agreement 72
Schuman Plan 152-3, 155
secularity xi, 5-7, 53, 54, 55-61, 65-6, 83, 126
Selim I 102-103
Selim II 104, 107
Selim III 110
Serbia 110-113, 115, 145
Sèvres, Treaty of (1920) ix, 13, 15, 82, 123, 167
Sezer, Ahmet 28, 36
Sicily 133
Sinan 107
Soviet Union 12, 14-21, 116, 123, 129, 132, 146, 151-7, 167
Spain 4, 88, 131, 136-7, 139, 141, 158
Spinelli, Altiero 150
Stalin, Joseph 153, 169
Suez Canal 113
Süleyman 36, 93, 96, 101, 103-4, 107
Sunni Islam 6, 56-7, 103, 193g
Superior Electoral Council (YSK) 33
Sweden 6, 69-70, 76, 158
Switzerland 69
Syria 14-15, 17, 24, 57, 79-84, 103, 107, 110-6, 121

taksim 175
Tamerlane 98-9
Tanzimat 11, 27, 194g

Tehran 23
Tel Aviv 22
terrorism 4, 21, 33, 62, 168–70, 175, 182
Thrace 96–7, 112, 115, 123–124
timar 98, 100, 105
treaties xi, 72, 82, 101–2, 107–115, 123, 141, 143, 146, 154, 155, 159
 see also individual treaties
Tunis 92m, 105, 107
Turkish Grand National Assembly 28

ulema 7
umma 12
United Nations (UN) 14, 22, 23, 154, 176, 179
United States (US) 69, 132, 139–40
 and Europe 21–5, 145, 151–4
 and Iraq 22, 155, 157
 and Turkey 14–15
USSR 12, 14–21, 116, 123, 129, 132, 146, 151–2, 155, 157, 167

Virtue Party (FP) 64
Venice 101–102, 105–106, 108
Verdun, Treaty of 137, 150
Vives, Luis 139

War of Independence 82–3, 125–6, 129
Welfare Party (RP) xi, xii, 19, 21, 29, 61, 63–4, 128
Western European Union (WEU) 154
westernisation 2, 6, 11–12, 63, 83, 119, 130
World Bank 43, 52
World Trade Organisation (WTO) 156
World War I 82, 83, 116, 120, 146, 150
World War II 14, 47, 119, 129, 132, 146–150, 161

YAS (Superior Military Council) 29–30
Young Turks movement 13, 115, 120, 165–7, 194g
Yugoslavia 129, 149, 153–4

ziyemet 58, 100, 104

www.ingramcontent.com/pod-product-compliance
Lightning Source LLC
Chambersburg PA
CBHW070534170426
43200CB00011B/2425